Small Groups in
Writing Workshops

Small Groups in Writing Workshops

Invitations to a Writer's Life

Robert Brooke
University of Nebraska–Lincoln

Ruth Mirtz
Florida State University

Rick Evans
University of Nebraska–Lincoln

National Council of Teachers of English
1111 W. Kenyon Road, Urbana, Illinois 61801-1096

Manuscript Editor: Humanities & Sciences Associates

Production Editor: Michael G. Ryan

Interior Design: Tom Kovacs for TGK Design

Cover Design: Jim Proefrock

NCTE Stock Number: 44837–3050

Library of Congress Cataloging-in-Publication Data

Brooke, Robert, 1958–
    Small groups in writing workshops: invitations to a writer's life /
  Robert Brooke, Ruth Mirtz, Rick Evans.
      p. cm.
    Includes bibliographical references and index.
    ISBN 0-8141-4483-7
    1. English language—Rhetoric—Study and teaching. 2. Forums
(Discussion and debate) 3. Small groups. I. Mirtz, Ruth, 1959–   .
II. Evans, Rick, 1951–   . III. Title.
PE1404.B753 1994
808'.042'0711—dc20   94-16963
                                       CIP

Contents

Acknowledgments

The authors gratefully acknowledge the help of many small and large groups who gave us invaluable encouragement, insight, and advice as we drafted and revised this book: The Composition Colloquium at the University of Nebraska–Lincoln, especially Kate Ronald, Joy Ritchie, Gerry Brookes, Tom O'Connor, and Bob Haller; Anne Whitney, Margrethe Ahlschwede, Judy Levin, Devan Cook, Jim Swingle, Mark McBride, and many other instructors at the University of Nebraska–Lincoln and Florida State University who read the manuscript or listened to our ideas; Michael Spooner, David Jolliffe, and the reviewers at NCTE; and the department staffs at both universities. We owe more than thanks to our spouses for their patience, support, and understanding.

Finally, we thank all the teachers and students who, with open hearts and minds, generously offered their stories and their writing to this project. This book is possible only through their belief that one person's experience can be valuable to many others.

I Principles

Introduction

This book provides a rationale, a set of principles, and some possible methods for using small groups in writing workshops. Using our students and ourselves as examples, we'll show how we've achieved success in using small groups to provide growing writers with the four essentials which we believe all writers need: time for writing, ownership over their topics and processes, ongoing response to their writing, and exposure to the writing of others. Small groups, we'll show, are an integral support to these four essentials, because weekly small-group discussions of drafts-in-progress surround growing writers with the response and exposure they need, while creating strong social pressure to maintain adequate writing time and to address the ownership issues of what to write about and why to write at all.

We were motivated to write this book by the questions we are continuously asked about small groups and teaching, by such diverse professionals as participants in the Conference on College Composition and Communication, new teachers of composition at the University of Nebraska and Florida State University, and secondary and elementary teachers we've worked with in the National Writing Project. Again and again, we've heard the same questions: "How often should my classes meet in small groups?" "How should I form the groups?" "How can I keep them on task?" Occasionally, we've even heard the most challenging question of all, "Why should I use small groups, anyway?" On the basis of our nine years' work with small groups in first-year and advanced writing classes, National Writing Project groups for practicing secondary and elementary teachers, faculty and graduate student colloquia, and our own collaborations as writers, we believe we have developed useful answers to these questions and have therefore written a book that meets a real need of teachers.

As we worked to develop our answers to these questions, however, we found we couldn't explain them easily through either the scholarly tradition of educational research or the textbook tradition of uncritical advice for teachers. In contrast, we discovered the principles and practices in this book through other methods: personal examination of our pedagogy, close participant observation in small groups of many kinds, and the careful construction of a learning environment which allowed for experimentation and second chances. As a result, much of this book is narrative. Because of these teacher-research methods, we found that we had collective and individual stories to tell about small groups, some of which we could write together using a group voice such as the one in this introduction. Other stories, though, seemed tied to the individual experience of our specific classrooms and needed, therefore, to be presented through our individual voices in order to illustrate our personal discovery and experimentation with each classroom, each small group, each of the assumptions we brought with us as teachers. Consequently, we've written some of the chapters in this book together and some as individuals.

Throughout the book, we will explain our answers to the questions we've been asked most frequently about small groups. We'll show why, for example, all three of us devote a third to a half of our class time to small groups, why we think the entire context of a class must be taken into account when addressing both global and local problems in small groups, and why we try to help individuals monitor their own group experience rather than trying to police what they do. Most of the second half of this book, entitled "Pedagogy," will examine what Ruth calls the "nuts and bolts" of our classrooms; most teachers will find their questions addressed there.

But we also believe that these "nuts and bolts" concerns only become significant in the context of a clearly articulated set of beliefs about how people learn to write and why we teach writing in the first place. Only some beliefs about writing and writing instruction imply the use of small groups. In fact, we think that there are good reasons why some teachers do not want to use small groups in their classrooms, as well as well-articulated rationales for teaching which argue against their use. Some teachers, we acknowledge, really ought not to use small groups at all because the beliefs they hold about writing don't match the opportunities small groups offer.

We *do* believe in the use of small groups, however. Our answer to the question "Why use small groups, anyway?" stems from our belief that writing is a social act, like speaking, and that learning to write happens most easily and most naturally in a conversational setting where writers dialogue with one another throughout the development of their pieces. Just as growing children learn oral language by trying to take part in the conversations around them—slowly developing competency over their language's structural rules through supportive interaction with peers and adults—so, too, growing writers naturally learn the purposes, uses, and rules of writing through trying to take part in the written conversations around them, aided by the supportive inter-action of peers and adults. In the first part of this book, entitled "Prin-ciples," we show why we hold these particular beliefs about learning to write and what they imply about students' experiences in small groups.

We encourage you, our readers, to use this book on the basis of your own beliefs about writing and your own pedagogical needs. If you are unfamiliar with the rationale behind student-centered pedagogies—for example, the work of Nancie Atwell, Lucy Calkins, Donald Murray, and the National Writing Project—then we encourage you to start with chapter 1, which places our approach in relation to the field of compo-sition as a whole. If you are somewhat familiar with this approach to the teaching of writing, you might prefer to start with chapter 2, which documents the particular challenges that we've found our students face when working in small groups, or chapter 3, which invites you to ex-plore your own reasons for being attracted to (or fearful of) small-group work by examining the background and experiences which led each of us individually to emphasize small groups in our own teach-ing. If you have been working with writing workshops for some time and really want some ideas for new ways of managing the "nuts and bolts" of small groups in your classes, you might want to jump in some-where in part II, perhaps into chapter 7's question-and-answer session, which covers the questions we've most frequently been asked about small groups, or perhaps into any one of chapters 4, 5, or 6, where each of us describes the most important features of our own classrooms. While we believe all the information in this book is important for fully understanding the principles and methods of successful small-group pedagogy, we encourage you to use the structure of the book in the same way that we encourage our students to use our advice about groups: as suggestions to try out, think about, reflect on, and consider as you identify your own beliefs about writing, your own ideas about teaching, and your own needs from small-group interaction.

1 Invitations to a Writer's Life: Guidelines for Designing Small-Group Writing Classes

Robert Brooke
University of Nebraska–Lincoln

It's 8:32 a.m., mid-February, and I'm fumbling with keys at my office door, trying not to spill the large toasted coconut coffee I've carried over from the Union. Arnold (twenty years old, John Lennon glasses, the first week of what will be a beard beginning to grow in) is already waiting outside my door.

"I wanted to show you the pen I bought," he says once we get inside my office. "I was reading Natalie Goldberg [*Writing Down the Bones*] last night, where she says you need to consider the kind of tools you use, you know, what kind of pen and notebook makes you feel like writing, so I went down to Nebraska Bookstore and bought three different fountain pens. Neat, huh?"

He hands me a bright green cartridge pen with a gold clasp, and he beams.

"I tried all last week to write two hours a night after my roommate went to bed, but it isn't working," Arnold continues. "He keeps having his girlfriend over, and they stay up really late watching TV. So, instead, I think I'll try writing whenever I can between classes and at work. How do you fit your writing time in? You always seem so busy."

—Excerpt from Robert Brooke's
teaching journal

I remember that very first workshop, which you led to get us started, got me off on the idea of how others influence our lives. I started out with just thoughts that went in no particular direction, and that eventually became a short little piece, only about half a page, but I explored the idea a little more, and was later able to use that as a start for a poem. It's weird how that took so long to take off. I kept telling myself I would start the poem, I would look at the short piece I had written, and felt absolutely nothing. But I knew I had to put this in a poem. One night I just sat down and wrote it, and somehow the thoughts found their way out, more clearly and concisely than I remember them filtering through my head. I remember looking down at the page and thinking that was what I needed to say, there were the thoughts expressed so that I fully un-

derstood them. I think I realized that I had to explain things to myself before I could explain them to someone else.

—Excerpt from a student's final
learning letter

I think the source of the most personal gain through this class was
in the small group discussion of works in progress. Through the
group I was able to refine my own writing through feedback, but
they did more than just that. The group experience helped me develop a critical eye and combine that with a constructive attitude
in voicing my criticism. I also learned a great deal about being prepared not only with materials, but with discussion of materials. It
is up to the writer to keep things moving along. That can often
mean that you, as writer, must articulate your concerns about the
piece and keep the discussion moving toward that goal.

—Excerpt from a student's final
learning letter

In the field of composition, what we want to happen when students
take writing courses is a topic of significant debate. The answer everyone seems to agree on is that we want our students to become better
writers; the debate emerges when we try to define what the phrase
"better writers" means. As I view the profession at present, this phrase
takes on several overlapping definitions. To cite just four: David
Bartholomae (Bartholomae and Petrosky 1986; 1990) and his colleagues
at Pittsburgh argue that "better writers" means writers who have become members of academic communities, who are able to write pro-
fessionally in college and for college audiences. Linda Flower (1982)
and John Hayes and their colleagues at Carnegie Mellon argue that
"better writers" means writers who are more conscious of their writing
processes and who are more able to manipulate the elements of that
process to meet any given rhetorical situation. Richard Haswell (1991)
of Washington State University argues that "better writers" means
writers who are maturing developmentally toward the organizational
and stylistic features of competent writers' prose. And researchers as
diverse as Kenneth Bruffee (1984), Ann Berthoff (1982), and Peter
Elbow (1981) argue that "better writers" means writers who are able to
use writing to understand their lives and their learning, and who are
able to use writing as a means of participating in ongoing discussion
with other writers.

All of the definitions of "better writers" have consequences for the
design of writing classrooms. The sequence of activities, the kinds of
writing students do, and the evaluation procedures used will all differ
depending on which definition a teacher employs. The choice to use
small groups as part of writing pedagogy is one of the items that de-

pends on a teacher's definition of "better writers." Given their definitions, for example, both Bartholomae and Haswell have proposed programs which argue against the use of small groups in writing classes.
The argument from Pittsburgh is that peer response from people who
do not understand the conventions and purposes of academic discourse can't help students grasp these matters. Haswell's argument is
that developing writers need individualized sequences that respond to
organizational and syntactic problems and that a knowledgeable
teacher is the best person to diagnose an individual's needs and design
these sequences. The choice to use small groups in a writing class,
therefore, isn't just a methodological choice between equal means of
getting across the same information—it's a choice that derives from the
way a teacher defines the "better writers" she wants her students to become, from the goals of her teaching. Writing groups function well
when they are an integral support to one's teaching goals, but they are
bound to be frustrating when they are peripheral or even opposed to
those goals.

Ruth, Rick, and I have talked a good deal about the goals of our
teaching and about the ways small groups provide essential support
for those goals. What's emerged from these discussions is a tentative
consensus on the way we define the "better writers" we hope our students will become. I articulate our consensus this way: we want our
students to understand writing as a lifelong practice, especially as a
means of reflecting on their experience and their learning, on the one
hand, and as a means of participating more fully in the communities
they are a part of, on the other. To be "better writers" means, for us, to
understand the ways in which writing can be useful in many areas of
one's life, as well as to have experiences which adapt writing to any of
those uses.

Such goals, I think, bring the three of us closer to the Flower and
Hayes or Berthoff and Elbow goals of our profession than to the
Bartholomae and Haswell goals. I know this is true in my case. I am attracted to Flower and Hayes's emphasis on knowing how to manage
the problems and processes of writing across rhetorical contexts, to
Berthoff's emphasis on writing as a means of discovering how one's
mind makes sense of one's world, and to Elbow's emphasis on writing
for multiple purposes throughout life. I frequently cite the following
passage from Elbow's recent "Reflections on Academic Discourse"
(1991a) when I find myself in discussion with university colleagues and
am asked to explain my pedagogy:

> [T]he best test of a writing course is whether it makes students
> more likely to use writing in their lives: perhaps to write notes and

letters to friends or loved ones; perhaps to write in a diary or to make sense of what's happening in their lives; perhaps to write in a learning journal to figure out a difficult subject they are studying; perhaps to write stories or poems for themselves or for informal circulation or even for serious publication; perhaps to write in the public realm such as letters to the newspaper or broadsides on dormitory walls. I don't rule out the writing of academic discourse by choice, but if we teach only academic discourse we will surely fail at this most important goal of helping students use writing by choice in their lives. (136)

I want my students to see the usefulness of writing throughout their lives and to be self-aware enough to make appropriate use of writing when the situation calls for it.

These goals for our teaching arise, no doubt, out of our own and our students' past experiences. Our personal stories of growth into writing groups (chapter 3) will show the ways we've used writing as reflection on life's events and as participation in communities important to us. In many ways, our pedagogical goals arise directly from these aspects of our own lives. Our students, we've found, share many of these aspects. As we'll show in chapter 2, many students also experience a need for writing as a means of bridging the "private" sphere of deeply held opinions and the "public" sphere of open discussion, as well as a need for exploring the diversity that daily surrounds us all. In our talks at national conferences, we've heard these same student needs identified by teachers across the country, from large urban centers in the North and East, from private and public colleges, and from both coasts and the Midwest. In developing a pedagogy that meets our own needs as writers, we've thus found that we address many of our students's needs as well.

At the same time, our pedagogical goals have also developed from working with many different students at the University of Nebraska and the Florida State University, listening to the various ways these students feel alienated from writing, especially in academic settings. The majority of traditional-aged Nebraska students, for example, come to us having had three years of high school English courses and are able to write tidy, mostly correct Standard Written English (supported no doubt by home and community backgrounds where English is the dominant language and a good deal of practical writing and reading goes on [Roebke 1977]). They come to us expecting to study hard in college (but often without having had to study hard before) and understanding much of what is involved in taking lecture classes with multiple-choice final exams. Yet, perhaps because of these relative strengths in scholastic preparation, many of our students come to us alienated from their learning, unsure of what to make of the large and often impersonal college campus and of what place academic study will take in their lives. Other students, who come to us in their mid-twenties or thirties or forties from the urban centers of Omaha, Lincoln, Sioux Falls, and Kansas City, find that they are trying to commit energy and attention to schoolwork now, after spending several years in the work force, and feeling the same restlessness they used to feel in school while also feeling frustrated because the jobs and lives they've been able to find without a college diploma are not as rewarding as the ones they imagine for themselves. Still others come to the University of Nebraska–Lincoln from the Lakota or Sioux reservations within the state, or the Hispanic communities around Scottsbluff, or the ethnically diverse areas of North Omaha, or on sports scholarships from large cities on either coast. These students find themselves often baffled at the provincialism and ethnocentrism of the Nebraska campus, and often struggling, as a result, to build bridges between their own experience and the lives of their professors and classmates.

The alienation students can feel from university life is perhaps best indicated by university attrition statistics. According to statistics for the University of Nebraska–Lincoln, over 20 percent of our entering students drop out of college before their sophomore year; only 40 percent graduate within the traditional four years (with a rise merely to 50 percent in a fifth year); and an ever-growing number of undergraduate students (29 percent) now fit into the "nontraditional" category of older students who are trying college for a first or second time after part of a life spent following different drummers.[1]

Given these students and these demographics, our emphasis on writing as lifelong practice has emerged almost necessarily from the interactions in our classes. Our students are many and varied, but one consistent need is the need to connect the life of thinking, reading, and writing (the so-called "life of the mind") with the other lives they lead (lives of work, of farming or small city communities, of relationships with friends, loved ones, relatives).

The metaphor I have consequently developed for thinking about our courses is the metaphor of invitations to a writer's life. In our courses, we invite our students to try out a writer's life for a semester, to see what it offers and what its potentials are, so that they will leave having some experience from which to decide whether writing can enhance the lives they already live.

Obviously, in the metaphor of a writer's life, I'm not talking about the life of a publishing creative or freelance writer supporting herself financially by writing. I'm talking instead about a person, holding any job, who uses writing as a means of enhancing her life through reflection and participation. I mean the whole range of uses of writing Elbow lists in the passage quoted above: writing as reflection in diaries and learning logs and responses to reading; writing as participation in letters, editorials, creative and polemical pieces; and, when appropriate, professional or scholarly writing.

Small groups are an essential support for these goals for our students. In their interactions in small groups, students are able to explore their own possibilities for a writer's life through participation in a small community of writers; repeated attention to the effect of their words and topics on other people; reflection on their topics, writing processes, and the responses of their group; and observing the ways in which their group members choose to use writing within the contexts of their diverse lives. While class time consists of a range of activities besides small groups, we see small groups as an integral, necessary part of the invitation we offer to a writer's life.

In the rest of this chapter, I will characterize what I see as the essential elements of a writer's life, in order to suggest these elements as organizing principles for writing courses which emphasize small groups. But the point of part I of this book (this chapter and the two following it) is wider than an introduction to a single set of principles for teaching writing. The point is that the best teaching of writing emerges out of a sympathetic awareness of the lives of teachers and students. We teachers teach best when we understand our own past and present lives, when we understand something of our students' pasts and imagined futures, and when we've reflected enough on the differences between our lives and theirs to understand in what ways writing might support each of us in those lives.

Characteristics of a Writer's Life

If writing courses are to be invitations to a writer's life—to a life in which writing serves as a constant aid to reflection and participation—then they need to be structured around the essential elements of such a life. I have identified four such elements:

> *Time:* Writers set aside time for writing regularly, perhaps by journaling three or four times a week after the family has gone to bed, or by spending the first two morning hours of the average workday writing down important (rather than urgent) ideas, or just by filling a spiral notebook each month. In order to benefit from the reflective and participatory rewards of writing, people need to de-

velop writing rhythms that work for them, that make writing a habitual instead of occasional activity.

Ownership: Writers maintain ownership over their uses of writing. By and large, they choose the topics they will write about during their writing time. They decide when a piece is worth continuing, or when to crumple it and throw it out, or when it needs to sit in a drawer and gestate for five years. They decide what the purposes of their writing will be, from the self-help purposes of private journals to the political purposes of letters to their elected officials. And they decide how to fit in the writing their job requires of them among the other writing they do.

Response: Writers rarely write in a vacuum. Writers need response, need a community of other people with whom they can discuss their words. Responders can take many forms, from journal/reading groups who meet because all the members share an interest, to individual dialogues in letters or with journal partners, to political action groups, creative writing groups, even the editors and readers of published work. All such responders make writing more than a solitary act; they make writing a means of ongoing participation with others who are important to the writer.

Exposure: Writers give themselves regular exposure both to other people's writing and to other writers. They read often in material directly relevant to their work and their own writing, as well as material which introduces them to other kinds of writing. They talk with other writers about the processes of writing, sharing their own experiences and learning from the experiences of others.

These four essentials all function in one way or another for people who have made a writer's life part of the overall life they lead, from the computer programmer who writes science fiction in her spare time to the secretary who journals with his "Parents Without Partners" group. Because these elements are so prevalent in the lives of practicing writers, they need to become structuring elements in writing courses which seek to introduce students to such a life. For students for whom school writing often seems divorced from other uses of writing—for whom the private sphere of opinion and intimate conversation often seems separated from the public sphere of school and job interaction—these elements can provide a means of identifying and exploring the possible connections between these artificially separated areas of their lives.

I didn't come up with these four elements on my own, though they are certainly supported by my experiences as a writer and teacher. I've borrowed most of them directly from writing teachers and researchers who have studied what children need as they first develop into writers. In the studies Donald Graves and his colleagues conducted at Atkinson Academy on young children learning to write (Graves 1984; Calkins 1983), time, ownership, and response were identified as elements essential for such learning to occur. Calkins's narrative of children's growth in that project documents the significant gains first-through sixth-grade children make in writing when they are provided these elements. Since her study focuses on children very early in the process of learning to write, her book is a wonderful antidote to any colleague who assumes such a classroom would be "advanced" and that entering college students need to have "the basics" first.

Since the publications of Graves's and Calkins's reports in the early 1980's, the notion of time, ownership, and response as structuring elements for a writer's growth has taken on a wider life of its own. In her Shaughnessy Prize-winning *In the Middle*, Nancie Atwell (1987) uses these three elements to describe the developing structure of her writing workshop for middle school students, and she returns to these elements in order to refine them in her recent *Side by Side* (1991), aimed at kindergarten through twelfth-grade teachers. These elements also inform, in general, the classes designed by Linda Rief (1992) for junior high school students; by Tom Romano (1987) for senior high school students; and, to a degree, by Donald Murray (1985; 1990) for college students. There is a sense, then, in which the notion of time, ownership, and response as structuring elements of writing classrooms has been slowly moving through the entire curriculum over the past decade, from elementary to college classes. (I've added "exposure" to the list to make explicit yet another essential that is sometimes obscured but is tremendously important for my students.)

Since these elements appear to be essential at so many grade levels, I can't help but wonder if they might not turn out to be connected to the ways in which human beings naturally become writers. Atwell (1991) writes:

> [T]he processes I wrote about are not unique to eighth graders. Although I observed writing, reading, and learning among junior high kids, writing, reading, and learning are human activities that cut across age, ability level, and ethnic background. In terms of their language learning, middle school kids are not a separate species. All of us, ages four to ninety-four, want our reading and writing to be meaningful, to make sense, and to be good for something. And teachers of all ages and subjects want to sponsor authentic contexts for learning and respond to their students as individuals. (137)

When students need to be exposed to a writer's life—to be introduced to the rich possibilities that writing has for enhancing any kind of life—it may be that they then need the essential elements of time, ownership, response, and exposure, no matter what their academic or age level. Although these elements consistently need to be adapted to the particular students, teachers, and contexts in which they appear, they may prove to be ideas that can organize the curriculum, kindergarten through college.

The profession of English studies is recognized by many scholars as now being in the midst of a profound paradigm shift, as throughout the field more and more competing specialties arise with more and more competing ideas about what is essential to English classes. I am heartened, therefore, whenever ideas appear that seem to make sense to teachers across the English curriculum. Such ideas are worth a careful look. And points of consensus do, occasionally, seem to arise. In the most recent national attempt to carefully reexamine the whole of the English curriculum—the 1987 English Coalition Conference sponsored by the Modern Language Association, the National Council of the Teachers of English, and several other organizations—many of the kindergarten through college-level teachers gathered there arrived at a kind of consensus about the essential goals of English instruction.[2] Writing with surprise at the general consensus he found emerging from such a diverse assemblage of teachers, Peter Elbow reported that

> [t]he way of talking that probably best sums up this idea for all participants is this: learning involves *the making of meaning and the reflecting back on this process of making meaning*—not the ingestion of a list or a body of information. At all levels we stressed how this central idea is deeply social. . . . In short, the main conclusion of the conference may be that we see the same constructive and social activity as the central process at all levels of the profession of English. (1991b, 18)

Of course, the particular ways teachers at different levels spoke of this consensual idea reflected their different contexts:

> There was a constant refrain from elementary and secondary teachers on the need to get students to be habitual writers and readers; only then can we be effective at getting them to be reflectors and examiners of language.
> Virtually everyone acknowledged repeatedly that the main practical finding of the last ten or fifteen years' renaissance in composition has been that students (and teachers!) should engage in more writing—even in class. This movement has taught us that we can't teach writing by just looking at models of others' writing or even by just talking about our own writing process: we have to

> emphasize production—the practice of writing—and devote
> plenty of time to this oddly neglected practice.
>   Similarly, college people stressed repeatedly that we should
> focus not on asking students to study theory as a content but on
> using theory as a lens through which to look at our actual reading
> and writing. Implicit here is the need to get people to engage with
> a text. (19–20)

I cite the documents of this conference at this length for two reasons:
first, because the tentative consensus arrived at does hint at the possibility that English teachers across grade levels can be validly working
with aspects of the same ideas; and second, because this particular conference's consensus emphasized regular engagement in and reflection
on writing and reading—an emphasis that comes close to supporting
the elements of time, ownership, response, and exposure which I've
identified above. Elbow's call for students to become "habitual" writers and readers and for classes to "emphasize production" seems to me
a recognition of *time* as a need. Similarly, for students to become "engaged" with texts, for them to reflect back on their production of writing and their interpretation of reading as a primary means of learning,
also seems an acknowledgment of the need for *ownership* over the purposes of writing, reading, and learning, and for *response* that helps individuals reflect and engage more forcefully. And the emphasis on
habitual reading and on the conscious uses of theory in reading and of
process in writing seems a substantiation of the need for *exposure* to
many different types of writing and writers. I am heartened to see evi-
dence in the reports of this national conference of ideas that seem trans-
latable into the elements of time, ownership, response, and exposure
which I believe are so crucial to my students' development as writers.

The elements of time, ownership, response, and exposure, moreover,
almost inevitably imply the use of small groups in writing classes.
Small groups provide writers with all four of these elements, either directly or indirectly. Obviously, groups provide writers with direct response—that's what groups are set up to do: individuals meet, read
their texts to each other, and talk about their reactions. But groups also
provide direct exposure to other kinds of writing and to other writers:
when individuals see the various kinds of writing other people attempt, when they see the uses to which other people put writing, and
when they can talk with others about the rewards, problems, and
blocks that emerge in the process of writing such pieces, they receive
wide exposure to aspects of writing outside their own experience.

Where small groups provide response and exposure directly, they
support time and ownership indirectly. People don't usually spend

time writing their own pieces while in groups—they have to find time for writing elsewhere during the week. But, for people who may be unaccustomed to writing as a habitual activity, the existence of regularly scheduled small-group meetings creates an artificial stimulus for making time to write. In my classes, the need to have a substantial piece of writing to read aloud to a group every Thursday creates a demand for writing time during the week; this demand is an indirect support for making the time necessary to write part of one's life. Groups likewise supply indirect support for the ownership element of a writer's life. From seeing the range of choices that others make in what they write, from needing to make personal decisions about the often conflicting and complex responses groups provide to writing, and from discussion of the many uses and processes of writing engaged in by group members, any individual's range of writing widens, providing more options, more choices, and hence more ownership over the writing he or she does.

Small groups, then, are not just an arbitrary method for classes that serve as invitations to a writer's life. They are an essential method, an integral support to the elements of time, ownership, response, and exposure. In the rest of this chapter, I'd like to focus a bit more on these elements and the role they play in my writing classroom.

Time

Of the four essentials of a writer's life, *time* is the one element teachers can't provide students within the college curriculum. In classes that meet twice or thrice a week for about an hour, it's become nearly impossible to provide sufficient, regular chunks of time for student writing. Even when teachers devote an entire class period to individual writing, they end up providing only about an hour per week. When I think of time as an essential for writers, I find myself envying elementary teachers who meet with students five days a week for several hours a day—in their situation, I could follow their lead and block out regular, daily in-class time for writing.

As it is, in the limited setting of the college class schedule, time is the single essential students need to provide on their own. In my classes, I make explicit the need for time and then confer with students individually to help them identify ways in which they can make regular time for writing in their busy lives. Small groups become indirect aids for establishing regular time, because each student needs to bring a substantially new piece of writing to the group each week and because in groups, students often talk about time-management issues. But each student still needs to make time for writing outside of class. For some students, this means tackling head-on the serious problem of scheduling their lives so that they can protect the same six hours each week for writing; for others, this means carrying small notebooks with them, so that they can write for fifteen minutes here and there when it's slow at work or when there's a break between classes; for still others, who by personality resist any attempts at scheduling hours during the week, this means setting other goals for themselves that imply time spent writing (for instance, setting a goal of writing ten new pages each week, some of which they will be ready to share in their group).

In each of these attempts to make time for writing, students are repeating the same strategies I see over and over again in the testimonials of professional writers, for whom the need for time often gets discussed in terms of the rhythms they create for writing in their lives. Donald Murray, who has collected many testimonials supporting the essential need for time in writing as an aid to discovery (see Murray 1978), writes of his own need for almost rigidly scheduled writing times: he spends the first morning hours of each day doing his own writing, hours he consciously protects (see Murray 1985). Joan Didion (1968) writes of the notebooks she keeps with her, writing down ideas or images as they strike her, claiming that this practice is useful both for clarifying her own experience as well as for the indirect support it gives her professional work. And Natalie Goldberg (1986) describes her practice of contracting with herself to fill a notebook with writing each month, not worrying too much about when or where it gets filled— sometimes, she confesses, this means that she gets to the 25th of the month with most of a notebook yet to fill and that subsequently she spends a whole weekend writing. But most of the time, she finds that this method leads to daily writing without the stress of fixed writing hours. These are the same strategies my students endlessly come up with: their ways of managing the rhythms of their writing lives end up being the same as those of our culture's professional writers.

What's equally interesting is that students discover things about the regular practice of writing that professional writers have often articulated. Roger, a junior-level student in one of my classes last year, wrote at midterm:

> I believe the most important progress I am making is with the time aspect of my writing. Although I am not fully locked into a writing time of my own, I am past the last minute production that I entered the course with. This is to me the most important concept I have encountered in the course. Without spending regular time with pen

and paper, the writing process can never get out of the blocks. Peer groups can offer little help if there is no time spent on writing.

At the end of the semester, he continued in much the same vein:

> When I left a specific time slot open for my own writing time, my writing did improve. I was able to explore many different approaches to the pieces I was working on. This allowed me to dance around a subject until I actually got to the meat of what I had deep inside.

In these passages, Roger identifies regular writing time as a "most important concept" because without it, the writing process can't operate. He goes on to write that, for him, the writing process requires a slow circling around his subject through a number of different approaches until the essential ideas—the "meat"—emerge. Roger here sounds remarkably like Kurt Vonnegut:

> [Novelists] have, on the average, about the same IQs as the cosmetic consultants at Bloomingdale's department store. Our power is patience. We have discovered that writing allows even a stupid person to seem halfway intelligent, if only that person will write the same thought over and over again, improving it just a little bit each time. It is a lot like inflating a blimp with a bicycle pump. Anybody can do it. All it takes is time. (Qtd. in Atwell, 1987, 56)

Both Roger and Vonnegut present images of writing as a slow, time-intensive process, a process in which their ideas are refined. Time, for both student and professional, is the key to this process.

Peg, a student who spent her semester splitting her time between private journals and public pieces for her group, wrote of a different outcome of regular writing time:

> I have come to understand what my reason for writing is, or who I write for: ME!! Past experiences caused me to feel the need to write well, or on certain things, for a grade, or for my peers, or as entertainment to the class. Now I understand and know that if those things happen, that's fine, but if they don't, that's okay, as long as I have learned and grown and benefitted from what I've written.

Peg's emphasis on the personal benefit of regular writing sounds here remarkably like the emphasis of Natalie Goldberg, who writes, in *Writing Down the Bones* (1986), that

> [o]ne of the main aims in writing practice is to learn to trust your own mind and body. . . . One poem or story doesn't matter one way or the other. It's the process of writing and life that matters. Too many writers have written great books and gone insane or al-

coholic or killed themselves. This process teaches about sanity. We
are trying to become sane along with our poems and stories. (12)

For both Peg and Goldberg, it's the personal rewards of greater self-un-
derstanding and greater sanity that most result from regular writing.
Good products ("A" papers; published poems) are an important by-
product of regular writing practice but not the energizing reason for
writing. In short, as these comparisons between Roger and Vonnegut,
Peg and Goldberg, show, in exploring time as an essential element of a
writer's life, students arrive at the same sorts of insights about themselves and their writing that professional writers have long described.
They explain how time spent on regular writing improves both the
writer's product and the writer's life.

Ownership

The second essential element of a writer's life is *ownership*, a term
which refers to the choices writers have over their material, their
processes, as well as how they understand and feel about their material and processes. People who write regularly usually write for a number of different purposes, from their own private notebooks, to their
writing on the job, to letters to friends and business associates. In managing their writing, they exercise ownership when they choose what
kind of writing to do at what times, when they reflect on their writing
to identify blocks they are having and to devise strategies for overcoming them, and when they develop ways to keep themselves engaged in writing tasks which have become stale but which they still
want to complete. In all of these areas, writers have control over many
choices, and it's that feature of choice which is highlighted by the essential element of ownership. Ownership, obviously, is complex, because it doesn't reflect the spoiled adolescent's attitude of "I'll do only
what I want to do when I want to do it," but more the reflective adult's
control over multiple choices for how to use writing in a world where
some kinds of writing are required by job, family, friends, politics,
while other kinds of writing are more individually motivated.

Roger, the student who wrote so much about time in his learning letters, identified the complexity of ownership at another point in his
writing:

I have realized the importance of ownership in the writing process.
Yes, a teacher could have directed my writing when I became frustrated at trying to find a subject and a style that I felt suited me. I

think it is more important that I had a chance to explore and discover what concerned me. It inevitably helped me to look at my writing, no matter how frustrated I was. I think it is likely that an assigned subject would not have focused my writing. I attempted to do so myself by dictating to myself that I would write poetry NOW and choose a subject. That decision went by the wayside after a few lines and I realized that I was not in the mood to try writing poetry at that time. So, I moved on to other things.

Roger puts his finger on the major complexity of ownership: the problem of frustration. Writers feel frustrated because of both too much and too little ownership. Roger became frustrated with himself both when he was "trying to find a subject that suited me," as well as when he assigned himself a poem on a particular subject and soon found that choice too restrictive. Like Roger, writers can become frustrated when the available choices over what they might do with writing seem so vast as to be overwhelming—they feel too much ownership over these choices and lack strategies for choosing between them. Like Roger, writers can also become frustrated when they feel the range of choice has been so narrowed that they don't feel any ownership over the writing—they feel too little ownership and lack strategies for making the writing personally engaging. These twin feelings of too much and too little ownership lead to frustration, a frustration which highlights that ownership isn't essentially a matter of choice over the topic: ownership, instead, involves an awareness of how to manage the many processes of writing that a writer engages in; an ability to devise strategies to overcome frustrations that appear whether a given writing seems to have too much or too little definition; and a recognition of the opportunities for choice that the writer has in each of these situations (for it's at those points of choice that the writer can make the writing her own). As Roger points out, having his teacher take ownership away from him by assigning him a topic wasn't the answer, because it was "more important that I had a chance to explore and discover what concerned me." Roger was aware that what he needed were strategies for developing personal engagement with his writing, and that such strategies would prove, in time, more important than any artificial narrowing of the choices he was making about his writing.

Ownership, in short, is a complex idea for writers, extending far beyond the usual meaning of ownership as the possession of property with which you can do what you like. That meaning doesn't really work for writing. In writing, it isn't enough to say "choose any topic you want and do with that topic whatever you want." In writing, ownership also involves the attitudes you take toward the writing you do, both "assigned" and "unassigned," and the strategies you employ for making whatever writing you do personally engaging.

In *Side by Side*, Nancie Atwell writes that she has reconsidered the term "ownership" for this essential element, wondering if the connotations of the word don't lead to unrealistic implications. If she were to rewrite *In the Middle* now, she says:

> I would never have used the word *ownership*. Students' *responsibility* for their writing and reading is what I sought, not control for its own sake. I worry that I helped readers infer that in order for students to take ownership of their learning, the teacher has to abdicate ownership of his or her teaching, lower expectations, and let students' choices rule the workshop. . . . My expectations of my students were enormous, and sometimes my nudges were, in fact, assignments to individual students: "Here, now try this." . . . The problem with ownership is the implication that any direction or assignment from the teacher is an infringement on students' rights. . . . When Tom Newkirk wrote to me about *In the Middle*, he said that for him the key term is *engagement* rather than ownership. (1991, 149–50)

Atwell, from the vantage point of five years' distance from her earlier work, suggests two alternative terms for the essential element she had called *ownership: responsibility* and *engagement*. These two terms certainly express aspects of what students like Roger are going through. Roger does feel responsible for his writing. He feels responsible for the choices of genre and topic he is making; he feels even more responsible for the way he is managing his writing time; and he describes significant learning about the practice and uses of writing at the same time as he describes some frustration with the products he produced. Similarly, Roger does express engagement with his writing—he is deeply engaged in the search for the kinds of writing "which suit him," even when he finds himself frustrated with particular pieces of writing. And, in his repeated attempts to write poetry and his repeated "dancing around" the same subject from different approaches, he shows definite engagement in particular genres and particular topics, even when he feels that he hasn't yet finished a product that does justice to his engagement. Responsibility and engagement are certainly key aspects of Roger's experience, necessary additions to his concerns with topic choice and genre.

The essential element of a writer's life that I've identified as *ownership*, thus, derives from writers' needs to be engaged with their work, to be able to identify the choices they have and devise strategies to help make those choices, to be responsible for the practice and product of their writing. Ownership in this sense is *owning the process* of your writing as much, if not more, than owning the more narrow choices of topic and genre. Writers own their products, if at all, in very odd ways, but owning the practice of writing, in all its complexities, is something essential to the workings of a writer's life.

Response

The third essential element of a writer's life is *response*. People who use writing in their lives usually surround themselves with responders to their writing. Such responders can take many forms: from the official editors and reviewers for published work, to the various writing groups where writing is shared (see Gere 1987), to support groups which recommend journal writing or political action groups which jointly produce newsletters and pamphlets, to letter writers. All of these kinds of responders engage writers in discussion about the ideas they present. Some, but not all, of these responders also talk directly about the form and effectiveness of the writing itself.

Writers need response to their writing for three reasons. First, getting response to writing brings the writer into a kind of community where writing is valued. Discussion of the ideas a writer is wrestling with, no matter how little they seem connected to the text itself, creates a context where the writer's ideas have social value. Second, through listening to the responses of others to their writing, writers learn about the reactions of other people, about the various ways different minds make sense of the same passages and deal with the same writing problems. Such learning helps them become better able to predict their readers' reactions while they write and improves their writing processes, as well. Third, response to particular drafts can often help writers see new possibilities and problems in their pieces, often leading to revisions that significantly improve the writing. Response provides new ideas for managing the problems a writer faces and models alternative ways for thinking about the text. In short, response to writing does more than just "fix" the writing by catching errors the writer has made in content, organization, or editing. Instead, response helps writers develop the feelings of social approval necessary to continue writing, an understanding of audience reactions and their own writing processes, and the ability to revise particular pieces effectively.

The experiences of my students Peg and Roger highlight these multiple purposes for response. Peg found the social-value purpose of group response to be the single most important precursor to her writing. For her to really begin to work as a writer, she needed to feel that the writing she was attempting had value for those she worked with: "It really surprised me how much the people made a difference to me," she wrote in her final learning letter. "Because my second small group felt or behaved a lot like I do, and because we all had writings that were pretty emotional, it was loads easier for me to break the separation I had with the personal/public writing." Writing became something she wanted to do once she found herself in a group with others who were using writing for the same purposes as she—once she found, in short, social approval for what she was attempting. Roger, by contrast, most valued the way the group experience helped him learn new strategies for dealing with writing in the future: "Through the groups, I was able to refine my own writing through the feedback, but they did more than just that. The group experience helped me develop a critical eye and combine that with a constructive attitude in voicing my criticism." While Roger noticed that the group feedback did improve his drafts, he stated in his final learning letter that he wasn't, in the end, pleased with his writings that semester. He found that problems still remained and that the groups hadn't helped him overcome all of them. Yet, he wasn't displeased with his group experience. Instead, he felt that the groups had helped him achieve a more important purpose in improving his ability, in general, to critique his own writing and to comment on the writing of others. The groups had improved his critique strategies perhaps more than they had improved any given piece he'd written. For both Peg and Roger, then, the short-term task of "fixing" individual drafts proved less important than more long-term concerns: finding that there was social value to certain kinds of writing because other people also used writing in the same ways; finding that one's abilities to critique writing generally improved through repeated group discussion.

Once we teachers recognize that response to writing serves all three purposes, both short and long term, it then becomes obvious that we need to provide many different kinds of response in our classrooms. To meet the short-term goal of helping to improve the specific texts our students write during the semester, we do need to provide response that highlights the strongest parts of drafts, points out potential problems in them, and makes suggestions for what the writer can try next. But this isn't the only purpose for response; if it were, then there would have been no need for the field of composition as a whole to critique the current-traditional practice of correcting student essays with marginal "awks" and "comma splices" as the only form of response in writing classes. Rather, since response also helps develop the writer's own strategies for writing and the writer's sense of the social value of her work, our classes need other response opportunities, as well.

I suggest that writing classes need to provide, at minimum, the following kinds of response regularly during the semester:

1. To meet the short-term goal of improving individual texts, writing classes need to provide response from other writers, response that provides direct suggestions for how and why the students might develop their texts further. Such response should come from several different writers, including the writer of the piece herself (as writer most engaged with the text), the teacher (as a more experienced writer sharing some strategies that might work), and other writers in the class (as peers facing the same issues).

2. To meet the long-term goal of helping the writer develop more strategies for writing and a better sense of how readers respond to texts, classes need to provide:
   a. frequent opportunities for readers to describe how they read a text, presenting the "movie of their minds" (Elbow, 1981), so that writers can hear the differences in how minds read (and so that both writers and readers can practice becoming conscious of how their own minds read); and
   b. frequent opportunities for writers to reflect on the response they have received, to identify the kinds of advice and reactions they are getting, to speculate about what this means for their writing, and to formulate their own plans for what to do next. Together, these two kinds of response provide writers with the data and the opportunities with which to identify and practice new strategies and ideas they might want to incorporate into their own writing processes.

3. To meet the long-term goal of helping writers see the social value in the kinds of writing they are doing, classes need to provide frequent opportunities to discuss the ideas and purposes underlying the writing. Writers need opportunities to talk about the ideas they are writing about, to share stories about these ideas with other people, to hear how other writers are also exploring these ideas. Writers also need opportunities to talk about why they are interested in writing certain kinds of pieces, to share stories about these purposes with other people, and to hear how other writers are also exploring these purposes. Such discussion, while not directly about individual texts, does much to support the social

value of writing because it shows developing writers that other people are also involved in similar uses of writing.

Together, these kinds of response all encourage writers to develop an ongoing writer's life. Together, they create an ongoing social context for writing, a habitual practice of reflecting on one's own work and other's reactions, and an ability to use feedback to improve specific drafts.

Exposure

Exposure, the fourth and final essential element of a writer's life, is in part an extension of the social-value purpose for response. In the same way that open discussion of a writer's ideas and purposes gives social value to the writing and makes that kind of writing more appealing to the writer, so, too, positive exposure to the other people's ideas, purposes, and uses of writing can make new kinds of writing appealing. Writers need exposure to other writers and their writing in order to see what's possible, in order to widen the range of what they themselves might try.

A long-standing maxim in composition instruction puts it that writers learn to write by reading, that good writers develop by reading lots of different kinds of writing and after a while come to incorporate (and extend) aspects of what they've read in what they write. The idea behind this maxim is that writers learn much about writing by submerging themselves in the world of writing; we learn much about writing through a love of reading. To my mind, this time-worn maxim points toward the importance of exposure in a writer's life: writers develop best in an environment that is rich in literacy, where they are exposed to reading material of many kinds and, even more importantly, to other people who write and read frequently themselves. Such exposure helps us imagine ourselves as writers, helps us see the social value of literate activities.

In *In The Middle,* Nancie Atwell dramatizes the importance of exposure by using the metaphor of the dining-room table:

> [D]uring dinner one night Toby discovered that one of our guests actually read and, better yet, appreciated his favorite author. Long after the table had been cleared, the dishes washed and dried, and everyone else had taken a long walk down to the beach and back, Nancy Martin and Toby sat at our dining room table gossiping by candlelight about Anthony Powell's *Dance To The Music of Time.* This didn't help me appreciate Anthony Powell, but it did open my eyes to the wonders of our dining room table.

> It was a literate environment. Around it, people talk in all the ways literate people discourse.... And our talk isn't sterile or grudging or perfunctory. It's filled with jokes, arguments, exchanges of bits of information, descriptions of what we loved and hated and why. The way Toby and Nancy chatted, the way Toby and I chat most evenings at that table, were ways my kids and I could chat, entering literature together. Somehow, I had to get that table into my classroom and invite my eighth graders to pull up their chairs. (1987, 19–20)

In the same way that children whose families are engaged in writing and reading come to appreciate literate activities just by taking part in dinner-table conversation, so, too, growing writers need to be surrounded with literate talk. By hearing and taking part in such talk, growing writers come to recognize that other people are, in fact, excited by reading and writing, finding value in certain books and projects, and may come to realize their own interest in such activities, too. Since, given the current demographics on the average American family, we teachers can rarely expect the majority of our students to have grown up around a dining-room table as literature-rich as Atwell's, part of our course's invitation to a writer's life needs to be a semester-long exposure to "all the ways literate people discourse."

I see three main ways to bring this exposure into our classrooms. First we need to set aside some time for individuals to share writing and reading with the whole class and with small groups. Student writers need to hear from each other what sorts of things they do read and appreciate and what sorts of things they write. In our classes, this first kind of exposure occurs most often through public reading days, in which each person in class reads a section of his or her best writing aloud to the class. These days provide direct exposure to the writing other class members do and are well received. (Frequently, students tell me that though reading their own piece aloud is frightening, they really enjoy hearing what other people have written and hope we will do this often.) Ruth, Rick, and I have also experimented individually, in a variety of ways, with bringing outside reading into the classroom, from individual book talks on a writing the students admire, to open letters to the class about a group-selected reading, to full-class discussion of the same essay, story, or poem. All of these methods are ways to set aside time for individuals to share writing and reading with the class, functionally exposing class members to writing they wouldn't otherwise consider. Roger, for example, found himself attempting poetry in the second half of the semester, largely because of what he'd heard others try. As he put it, "Looking back on my own goals for this half of the term, I recall I hoped to make an attempt at writing poetry. I did do this. Hearing the poetry that others in class were able to produce, I hoped to be able to duplicate that feeling." It became possible for Roger to try his hand at poetry because other classmates read poetry aloud at full-class readings and for book talks, and he liked what he heard.

Second, small-group discussion of writing is an ongoing forum for exposure. Each time a group meets to share drafts or ideas, the members of the group are functionally exposed to three or four other people's interests in writing and reading, and they are likely to hear why the person wants to write the kind of piece she's writing and what sort of pieces this writing reminds her of. Group meetings consequently provide ongoing exposure to the literate activities that the group members value and participate in. In Roger's group, for example, this kind of exposure led Bill, a nontraditional student who'd come to school after a term of enlistment in the Navy, to a kind of writing he had never imagined before. While Bill's first pieces were attempts at traditional essays on the death penalty and motorcycle laws, Carl, one of his group members, brought in drafts toward a historical drama about the Civil War. Carl, it turned out, was involved in Civil War battle recreations at Fort Kearney in the summer, knew something about military writing, and shared his knowledge of military authors with his group as background to his writing. Within a month, Bill had embarked on his own military writing: a dramatic account of life aboard a Navy cruiser in the South Pacific.

Third, our own writing and reading as teachers provides direct exposure to the literate activities we value, and this exposure is often useful for growing writers who haven't spent much time with any adult who openly admits to a love of reading and writing. I regularly share my writing with my students, doing my own writing on the board on days when we write individually in class, sharing my writing with small groups on small-group days, and taking my turn on public reading days. Similarly, I share my reading with them as well, mentioning in groups the pieces I've read that their work makes me think of, and loaning these pieces to individuals when I have them in my private library (under the threat, if necessary, of a "No Report" if I don't get them back by the end of the semester). Our own behavior as teachers often provides a kind of model of literate activities that students can try out. Over the past two years, for example, while I've worked in class on a personal collage essay about a hiking trip I took with my father when I was ten years old, several students in each class have started writings that explore their own relationships with their fathers. With these students, I've then shared personal essays about father-son relationships from journals like *Georgia Review* and *Prairie Schooner*, only to find these essays—and some of the techniques they demonstrate—spreading as if by magic to comments in students' letters to me, to small-group discussions, and to the kinds of pieces other students attempt.

T. S. Eliot wrote that beginning writers borrow, but mature writers steal—an adage pointing humorously to the importance of exposure in literate life. Exposure to writers and writing is the final essential element of a writer's life that we try to emphasize in our classrooms, so that developing writers will have some taste of the rich world of reading and writing from which they can borrow or steal in the creation of their own purposes and uses for writing within the contexts of their own lives.

Conclusion

Time, Ownership, Response, and *Exposure* are elements of a writer's life which I consider crucial for our students. Taken together, these four elements surround developing writers, at least for a semester, with some of the tempos, issues, and discourses that make up writers' lives throughout our culture.

Small groups, as I've suggested, can be an integral means of providing these four elements to writing students. Small groups provide response and exposure, directly, and support time and ownership, indirectly. Since Ruth, Rick, and I have all decided that we want our teaching to help our students explore writing as a life practice, we've all found small groups to be important to our teaching because of their direct and indirect support of these essential elements of a writer's life.

As I've tried to present them here, time, ownership, response, and exposure are guiding principles that can be used in many contexts by teachers who want to teach writing as an invitation to a writer's life. I've tried in this chapter to present these principles as principles, out of the particular context of any single writing class, largely because Ruth, Rick, and I believe that there are many ways of making these principles operative in classrooms and that each teacher needs to design her own classroom in response to the needs of her students and her own past experience. Consequently, we believe that any single classroom must be uniquely structured, even if it is also based on principles similar to these four. Although we do share a guiding philosophy, the three of us don't teach in the same way. Every teacher, we believe, needs to be creative in designing writing courses that fit the philosophy, the students,

know each other from high school, and they sit and talk to each other during class, and don't bother to talk to me and the other guy.

Neal: Who's the other guy?

Adam: Oh, I don't even know. He hardly ever says anything. He studies his algebra most of the time during our small group. His papers are mostly about his family, his grandparents. I don't take my real writing to them, my short stories. We read each others' papers and then just sort of wait until class is over.

A new small group would be very good for me, because I am not motivated to do my best writing in the group I am in now. I think all new people would be best for me, but I honestly do worry what Ann and Kris might think because we've gotten to be good friends. Hmmm . . . Can I get in a different group without it being obvious that I wanted a new group? Or do they also want different groups?

> —Excerpt from a writing student's midterm note to her teacher, contemplating the possibility of changing group members

At first, I felt like I was in a group with a lot of people who did not want to be in the class. They all took it to fulfill requirements. And they all stated at the beginning of the class how they did not like to write. [But] by the time the first polished paper was due, they seemed almost excited to hand it in. They came with scrolls of computer paper. It made me excited for them.

> —Excerpt from a writing student's report to her teacher on what happened in her writing group

As Robert described in chapter 1, all three of us design our writing classes around the four principles of time, ownership, response, and exposure. Individual writers are responsible for making the time in their lives for continued writing and for choosing topics and genres which engage them. While our classes help them with these matters, especially with exploring possible ideas for writing, much of our class time is devoted to the third and fourth of these principles: response and exposure. Well over half of our class time is spent in activities derived from these two principles: students talk about their ideas for writing or their writing processes, respond to each other's ideas or the writing of published authors, and reflect on the meaning of their own and their peers' responses for their developing thoughts and texts. Some of these activities occur as full-class activities—for example, we hold public reading weeks during which each writer reads for ten minutes from the work she has completed. Some are individually completed and then shared in impromptu groups of two or three—we might each draw a lifeline on which we mark events, stages, important places or people we might want to write about, and then share an item from this lifeline with someone else in class. And some are completed in impromptu groups—we might ask groups of students to plan and lead a class discussion on an essay they choose from our reader or on an editorial from the university newspaper. Our classes are rich in response and exposure, as well as in the impromptu small-group interactions that support these principles.

But within this plethora of response and exposure, small-group response to drafts-in-progress takes a particularly important place. Our students meet once weekly in response groups to read aloud and discuss their writing. With some variation early in the semester, they meet with the same people in groups throughout the semester and give and receive a variety of written and oral commentary. The weekly group meetings by themselves take up a third to a half of our total class time, meeting one fifty-minute period each week on our Monday/Wednesday/Friday schedules and a good portion of one day each week on our Tuesday/Thursday, hour-and-fifteen-minute schedules. We also require students to write about their groups and the response they are receiving in at least three ways: by reflecting on what's occurred in their group at the end of each class meeting; by writing and sharing their thoughts on their group's processes with peers at several points during the semester; and by writing to us as teachers about the effects of their groups on their writing when they turn in learning letters that accompany their work at midterm and end of term.

Small-response groups are thus the most continuous, frequent, and monitored feature of our classes. By the time the semester is over, students have a lot of experience with them and have spent a lot of time reflecting on what happened in group and what it meant for their writing. Although we use impromptu small groups in many other ways throughout our classes, these weekly groups responding to drafts are what we and our students think of as small groups during the course of the semester.

In this chapter, we will describe some of the experiences that student writers have in these small groups. Response groups, we believe, present certain challenges for students, interactions which can help students grow as writers if they manage them well but which can become frustrating for them if they don't. Because response groups place students in discussion with others whom they might not otherwise talk to, because response groups create extended, semester-long contact with these people, and because the talk in response groups centers on the widely disparate material individuals are writing about, these groups challenge students to make sense of their own lives and work in relation to the lives and work of others. This is by no means an easy task.

In this chapter, we'll draw on our students' reflective writing to paint a verbal picture of the range of experiences students have in groups and of the consistent, ongoing challenges they describe to us year after year. We'll look first at ways students have described their group experiences, using their own metaphors of families, first dates, tools, and biker's bars. We will then develop three particular challenges that seem to arise frequently in groups: what to make of the public/private issues about writing and life that groups involve, the diversity of people in any group, and the conflicts group pedagogy confronts them with between past, present, and future educational experience.

Students' Metaphors for Small-Group Experience

For us, one source of insight into the various ways our students are experiencing their groups is the way they describe the group itself. When Ruth asked her students (during the 1989–90 academic year) to write metaphors about their small group, they captured in their metaphors some of the range of experience they feel. Because the metaphors they chose tend to emphasize the significant felt experience of being in the group rather than their sense of the group's task or accomplishments, their metaphors give us some insight into the mental models and past experiences that students use to interpret and evaluate their groups.

A significant number of students describe their small groups as friendly and family-like in their unconditional acceptance. Following are some of the metaphors students use to describe their small groups in this way:

> My small group is like . . .
>
> a family, because I can tell them just about everything without being all uptight.
>
> a class reunion. After the first few weeks of getting to know each other, we talked about more than just our papers, like what happened this week.
>
> being with friends. My small group got to be close and before we read our drafts we always visited about how our lives were. It was comforting to know that if you didn't make it to class someone cared.

These metaphors are about people other than classmates, all friends and family, suggesting that students have positive feelings about other small groups and interpersonal relationships in their lives. The students who wrote these metaphors made connections between the groups they had been in (such as circles of friends or their immediate family) and classroom groups they were more or less forced to be in. They also seemed to think that the other students in their group were somehow like them and shared out-of-class experiences with them.

Other students are more hesitant about what's going on in their small groups and about how the group members work together:

My small group is like . . .

meeting someone new because you never know for certain what responses you will get.

a group of conspirators because we gather and discuss things that only we hear that don't leave the group, at least . . . unless we decide to share by writing a speech on it or a major paper.

a first date, because you're nervous and don't know how you'll do.

These metaphors are more tentative; they seem to be written by students who weren't sure of whether they shared experiences and values with their small-group members. These students may not have been sure of how much to share, with whom, or when, suggesting real concerns with the public/privacy issues that arise in group discussion of self-chosen writing, and also suggesting past experiences where these same issues of privacy had been treated without tact by other people.

Another set of metaphors describes small groups as more utilitarian in emphasis:

My small group is like . . .

an electric shaver when it comes time to shaving, because it helps cut down the time of a tedious task. It is also very helpful especially if you don't want to cut yourself.

a set of jumper cables because it gets you going and helps you start new ideas.

throwing a ball up in the air because once you give them the paper they throw back feedback.

being on an athletic team; everyone helps each other reach a common goal.

These students saw their small groups as aids in the writing process but not as family. They didn't describe the small group as primarily a human relationship but as friendly assistance. There may be a notion of fundamental equality among group members here, similar to the family and friends metaphor, but it is focused on the feeling that if they all pitch in, the work will get done (which, of course, is a version of groups intimately related to past experiences with successful athletic teams, work groups, and life in families).

All of the preceding metaphors describe groups which generally manage to work things out, even though the relationships may be a little confusing or unusual. Most students who find themselves enjoying their small group tend not to see themselves as "stuck" in their group, in the same way that they don't feel "stuck" in their circle of friends or family or teammates or co-workers. Of course, they are not free to leave one group and join another (as they can with friends outside of class), but they can deal with conflicts and differences the same way they do in the other groups they belong to. For example, friends or family or teammates get along because they assume the best, most faithful interpretation of what their colleagues say and do; when they don't understand why a friend said or did something, they ask because they want to understand; and they recognize that people keep changing, which means that relationships between and among people keep changing, too—what works one day will not necessarily work the next. Students in small groups who see themselves as a functional family or team or set of friends seem to use the same accommodating and adapting behavior in the group that they use with their families, friends, and teammates.

However, not all small groups end up having positive experiences:

> My small group is like . . .
>
> watching Sesame Street after you've just seen a five hour documentary on cold fusion. I've worked in [a] small group setting like this many times before, and all of them were more profitable than this has been. I know that other groups excelled at helping each other, but there are some people who cannot naturally do this— they need to watch others do it first.
>
> me fitting in at a biker's bar.

Being in a small group in which the members do not get along, or one which doesn't seem to help a student's writing, is extremely frustrating for the students and teacher alike, especially when there doesn't seem to be any way of changing the group members or their behavior. Feeling like one doesn't belong or like the rest of the group is "just too weird" isn't unusual, according to some students' reports. When students find themselves "stuck" with people they either don't like, don't agree with, or don't respect, they may withdraw from participating in the group, just as they would withdraw from participating in a group outside of class which alienates them. Generally, withdrawing only makes the small-group experience worse, because then the other group members resent or fear the silence of one member. For students who find themselves in groups with people very unlike themselves, the past group strategies they bring to their group may not be enough. The interaction strategies that work for family and friends and teammates (the essential assumptions of good intentions based on past interaction) don't seem to hold up; the avoidance strategies that work in situations where a group seems totally foreign to them (leaving the bar once you've discovered it's a biker bar; finding a new church) aren't really possible given the arbitrary partnerships of classroom groups. Such groups directly challenge students' abilities to adapt, and sometimes the challenge is overwhelming.

To summarize, the metaphors Ruth's students provided show a range of felt experience in small groups, one which extends along a continuum from comfort to frustration. On one end are metaphors which describe small groups as friends and family (metaphors of closeness and comfort). On the other end are metaphors which describe small groups as unworkable blends of diverse people (metaphors of frustration and alienation). On points in between are the other sets of metaphors which describe degrees and blends of comfort and frustration (the group as a tool for getting the job done, the group as a tentative collection of people getting to know each other).

These metaphors show us that the emotional experience surrounding small groups is rich and complex, and that much of the character of this experience stems from the ways students are able to match their group interaction to other experiences they've had in the past. Clearly, to make sense of their writing groups, students rely on their past interactions in other groups, and much of the felt success or failure of their writing groups apparently depends on the degree of match they feel between past and present. The students who describe their groups as family may feel a correspondence between the writing group and important elements of their past. Students who describe their groups as tools to accomplish the classroom task of writing may feel a match between the writing group and other groups in their lives (for example, work groups rather than circles of close family or friends). Students who describe their groups as bikers' bars might feel themselves, by contrast, in a significant mismatch, as if their pasts have not prepared them for the personalities they now confront.

Latent in all these metaphors are three pervasive challenges students confront in dealing with classroom writing groups: (1) the question of what to do with the established patterns of interaction (and literacy) they bring with them, of what to make of the ways they normally do things, especially their established ways of managing public and private discourse; (2) the problem of diversity and individual differences, of the fact that other people (in the group, in class) seem to be operating in ways that make little sense or directly challenge the ways in which they act; and (3) the problem of educational context, of the arbitrary nature of the class's small groups and the complex ways this educational context does and doesn't match what they've experienced before in school. In the remainder of this chapter, we'd like to develop each of these themes a bit more.

What to Make of Established Patterns of Interaction

As writers, speakers, and group members, our students don't come to us with their minds a blank slate, waiting patiently for us to inscribe on them patterns of writing and group behavior. Instead, they enter our classrooms with minds already formed by their pasts, with established patterns of reading, writing, and oral interaction. One of the enduring questions individuals face in our classrooms is what to make of these patterns in the new context of college writing classes: Do the ways I've always written, read, and talked before hold true here as well? Or must I give up these up to be successful in college? Or, if I find that the ways of writing and talking in college are different from what I'm used to, are there ways of blending the two into something I can use both in and out of school?

These questions exist, tacitly or explicitly, in the metaphors we presented above. When students describe their groups as "family" or a "work team," they are expressing a feeling that some of the ways of talking, reading, and writing which they bring to class do, indeed, match what's expected in class. In exploring that degree of match, students are exploring these pervasive questions about what to make of their established ways of doing things in the context of the classroom.

Current linguistic and ethnographic research has gone to great pains to show that these enduring worries are based on real differences in interaction and literacy patterns in people's lives. Deborah Tannen's recent bestsellers on conversational style (see Tannen 1986; 1990) have done a tremendous service by explaining in layperson's terms the complexities that arise in oral interaction when conversational styles don't match, especially since her work consistently demonstrates that mismatches stem from unacknowledged differences in community norms for interaction:

> [O]ur personal worlds are shaped by conversation—not only with
> family, friends, and co-workers but also in public. Whether the

world seems a pleasant or a hostile place is largely the result of the cumulative impressions of seemingly insignificant daily encounters: dealings with salespeople, bank clerks, letter carriers, bureaucratic officials, cashiers, and telephone operators. When these relatively minor exchanges are smooth and pleasant, we feel (without thinking about it) that we are doing things right. But when they are strained, confusing, or seemingly rude, our mood can be ruined and our energy drained. We wonder what's wrong with them—or us.

Indirectness, ways of using questions or refusing politely, are aspects of conversational style. We also send out signals by how fast we talk, how loudly, by our intonation and choice of words, as well as by what we actually say and when. These linguistic gears are always turning, driving our conversations, but we don't see them because we think in terms of intentions (rude, polite, interested) and character (she's nice, he's not).

Despite good intentions and good character all around ... we find ourselves caught in miscommunication because the very methods—and the only methods—we have of communicating are not, as they seem, self-evident and "logical." Instead, they differ from person to person, especially in a society like ours where individuals come from such varied backgrounds. (1986, 12–13)

Because of the minutiae of our pasts, the many small conversations we've observed and taken part in, we develop characteristic ways of talking which make perfect sense in the communities from which we learned them, but which may seem slow, rude, pushy, aggressive, or passive to people from different backgrounds. In our patterns of oral language use, we act out of these established ways of talking, and the degree of match between these ways and the ways of those we interact with influences the felt sense we have of comfort or frustration.

The relationship is similar with written language. In recent years, ethnographers such as Shirley Brice Heath have shown that the uses of reading and writing vary widely from community to community and that the established ways of interacting with written language likewise vary. In her landmark study of two blue-collar communities in the Piedmont (Heath 1983), for example, Heath showed that both communities had clear, functional, and established ways of using and discussing written language, but that these ways differed so greatly from the ways in which local schools treated writing, that the children from these communities exhibited difficulty:

The different types of uses of reading and writing of Roadville and Trackton have prepared the children in different ways for negotiating the meaning of the printed word and the production of a written text. Children from neither community have had experi-

> ence in seeing their parents read or write extended pieces of prose.
> Both have concepts of print. Roadville's children have been
> coached in book-reading at bedtime and in sessions around the
> kitchen tables over coloring books. Trackton's concepts are unar-
> ticulated and unrehearsed. The children hold onto some perceptual
> antecedents of shape and style in the print on signs, cans, and
> newspapers. Roadville children come to school imbued with oral
> testimonies about the value of reading, but with few models of
> reading and writing behavior. Trackton children have not heard the
> activity extolled, but have seen numerous group debates over what
> letters, notices, and bills mean. Children of both communities have
> heard preachers and their adult friends and relatives speak from
> the written word in church, and they have come to know the lim-
> its of oral interpretation of these words. . . . The significance of
> these different patterns of language socialization for success in
> school soon become clear. After initial years of success, Roadville
> children fall behind and by junior high most are simply waiting out
> school's end or their sixteenth birthday. . . . Trackton students fall
> quickly into a pattern of failure. (348–49)

As in oral language, our past histories of observation and participation
in our communities' ways of using written language lead us to develop
patterns of literacy which function in our communities, but which may
not function as smoothly in other contexts such as school or work.

As people who later chose to become English teachers, most writing
instructors come from backgrounds where the ways of using writing
and speaking match to a large degree what goes on in school and college. Our colleague Kate Ronald, coordinator of composition courses at
the University of Nebraska–Lincoln, is quick to point out that, by sheer
population numbers, our ease as English teachers with the kinds of
writing and reading we do puts us clearly in a minority.

Obviously, as all the ethnographic work on communities' patterns of
talk shows, each geographic/ethnic/gender community will have different established patterns of interaction, which will conflict with college classrooms in unique ways. Many of these conflicts are reflected in
students' expressed worries semester after semester and in the teacher
"lore" (North 1987) about students at any given college. One worry our
students often express involves the tension between the writing and
speaking that they feel ought to be private and the writing and speaking that is public.

Peg, the student we quoted in chapter 1, explained these tensions in
characteristic fashion in her end-of-the-semester letter to Robert:

> Now for my goals [students met individually with Robert in weeks
> 4, 8, and 12 of the semester to establish individual goals for their

work]. When we met the first time, the goal I set myself was to keep a personal diary, and to write in it every night before I went to bed. That was meant to help me separate and deal with the public/personal conflict I felt in writing for this class. It was like I couldn't write what I wanted to write on for class, because it was too close to home or emotional or personal for me to share with my small group. So I kept this journal (and still keep it, and write in it at least three or four times a week even!!) to help me sort through my thoughts and then pick out what it was I was able or wanted to share with my classmates. That worked pretty well, although I do have to admit what helped even more was when we changed small groups. It really surprised me how much the people made a difference to me. Because the second small group felt or believed a lot like I do, and because we all had writings that were pretty emotional, it was loads easier for me to break the separation I had with the personal/public writing. So I met the first goal I had, not only from keeping a personal diary, but also by forming a close family within my group that I felt comfortable sharing things with.

For Peg, as for many of our students in Nebraska, the immediate way she experienced the clash between her own established ways of using speaking and writing and the class's emphasis on small groups was as a personal/public conflict. The work of the class felt to her as if it would take place on a very troubling boundary between the emotionally dense ways of interacting reserved for family and close friends and the supposedly functional and neutral ways of interacting reserved for school and work. The pieces she wanted to write in class emerged from the emotionally close arenas of her life (for Peg, these arenas were her large farm family and her church), but she feared the distanced, indirect, potentially analytical ways of talking about writing that she expected in her classroom small group.

Peg's struggle with the personal material she wanted to write and the public audience of the small group led her to want a group that she could think of as "family" and to feel isolated in her initial small group. Peg's experience with her first small group was un-family-like and potentially threatening. (This group included two older writers, one of whom had publishing experience, and both of whom treated group discussion from the first day as a place to make judgments about the writing and suggest revisions—even though Robert had advised the class to postpone judgment and revision suggestions during group interaction.) Consequently, Peg initially tried to handle the tension by dividing her writing into public and private realms. For the first half of the semester, Peg wrote in a private diary that no one else saw (she showed Robert that she had written in it, but even he did not read it) and brought in a piece developed from her journaling for small-group meetings. Like many of our students, Peg was not entirely comfortable with this resolution because she did, in fact, want to discuss the ideas and writings she was doing in her diary—but she wanted the discussion to follow supportive patterns.

When Peg moved after midterm into a second small group, she found what she was looking for in terms of interaction patterns, and she subsequently found herself using words like "family" more and more to describe her new group. Later, in her final letter to Robert, she expanded on this theme:

> We switched small groups, and after doing so, I realized how easy it can be to share personal writing, so after about two sessions in my new group, I felt perfectly comfortable with my writing, and didn't really separate it into personal/public categories. And what's really interesting is how that overflows into the whole class atmosphere or feeling I have towards sharing my work with the class. Case in point: I presented a very personal and religious and emotional song for the last class reading. I know damn good and well I wouldn't have even CONSIDERED sharing that after I read it to my first group. They didn't respond at all in a way that encouraged or helped or motivated me to work on it some more. But my second group did, and they in turn helped me realize, as did my own reasoning and writing, that I could share my writing.

What made the difference for Peg was the nature of the interaction in her second group. Where the interaction in her first group led her to establish a division between emotional/personal interactions and functional/public interactions, her second group consisted of people who, like her, were feeling the need to blur those divisions and have class time spent dealing with some of the emotional areas of their lives. Because in her second group "we all had writings that were pretty emotional," the nature of the interaction was different. She felt able to ignore the public/private distinction. She felt encouraged to revise more and write more. She described her new group as being like a "family."

Peg's case here is a kind of exemplar for one of the enduring questions faced by the students in our classrooms: What do students make of their established ways of interacting in speaking and writing, given the context of the classroom? Peg's experience shows some of the complexity of this question for students. For her, on the public/private division so many students experience, her interactions in writing and in groups were a consistent challenge to her (a challenge that, luckily for her, she was able to resolve). Many such divisions and challenges affect the learning of all our students.

Confronting Diversity

A second enduring challenge for our students is what to make of the diversity they find in their writing groups. Most of our students are likely to find in their classes and writing groups people who are very unlike themselves. There are huge differences between the farm, ranch, and city areas of Nebraska, even for traditional-age students who may at first seem to look homogeneous. In Florida, there are huge differences among the inner-city cultures of Miami with its Hispanic communities, the life of families in the coastal fishing industry, and the life on peanut farms in southern Georgia. Given as well the growing nontraditional student population and the number of student athletes recruited from distant cities, any student is likely to find herself in a group with people whose past lives bear little resemblance to her own.

How our students deal with this diversity emerges consistently as one of the central issues they face in our classes. As Peg's story suggests, many students are at a bit of a loss when they find their group members behaving in ways they didn't expect. Diversity becomes an issue for group members because there is a high likelihood that most groups will include people from very different backgrounds who hold opposing viewpoints, and this diversity is likely to spawn a range of open and tacit conflicts. One group Robert worked with in a recent sophomore class exemplifies these issues beautifully. The group consisted of four people, three women and one man. The three women were all Nebraska natives, one from a small ranching community and the other two from Omaha; two of the three were sophomores, the other a senior; the senior and one of the sophomores were in the same sorority house, the third woman lived in a dorm. There were enough individual differences between the three of them to keep things interesting, but what really started the fireworks was the man in the group. A nontraditional student, Frank had grown up in Germany, spoke fluent English with a slight accent, had tried college twenty years earlier (the late 1960s and early 1970s) but had dropped out because he found school too confining, and he subsequently spent several years living in a sort of retreat from civilization in the backwoods of Alaska. Almost in every trait one could think of (gender, age, language background, schooling, politics, etc.), Frank was different from the three women, who were often so aware of their differences from Frank that they ignored the differences between themselves.

Here's how one of the women, Anne, described the progress of the group, from the retrospective vantage point of the end of the semester:

> It is tough to describe this amazing small group with one word. I
> would like to save face and say that we came great lengths past the
> storming process, but I really don't think we did. First of all, we all
> behaved like a bad thunder "storm" whenever Frank entered our
> group. It's taken me a very *long* time to adjust, but I guess we have,
> so within the last 1–2 small group sessions we have hit the norm-
> ing process. . . . I think we could have come far without the under-
> lying tension of the Frank situation. I also think a lot of times we
> made it worse than it really was, at least I know I did. I just wanted
> the three of us because Frank was so different. Sue and I in the be-
> ginning tried several groups and we found Angie to be very easy
> to work with, fun, and had many good ideas. Sue and I paired up
> because we were in the same house.

According to Anne's report, the differences in the people in the group
was a constant source of difficulty throughout the semester, so difficult,
in fact, that she reified it with the label "the Frank situation." The group
struggled each meeting to define how it would deal with the three-one
split between the women and Frank, and this ongoing struggle led
Anne to place the group as still being in the "storming" stage of group
process.[1]

Anne's sense of her group is wonderfully corroborated in the written reflections of the group members. Once we had put all four of their
writings next to each other, we could see the problems caused by the
group members' individual differences and the ways in which these
problems exacerbated because of students' reticence to talk through
their conflicts openly. Each of the four group members had a different
desire for what should happen in the group: Anne wanted Frank to
leave the group, so that only the three women would remain; Sue also
wanted Frank to leave, but she also felt inhibited by Anne because
Anne was a senior in her sorority house—she felt she had to follow Anne's lead and therefore was doubly cautious of what she said in group;
Angie was angry at Sue because of Sue's open unwillingness to work
with Frank—Angie claimed that she and they would learn more from
Frank's presence precisely because he was different; and Frank felt the
group was aimless, not sticking to the point of the assigned group
work, but he nonetheless enjoyed talking with the women about their
lives. No wonder Anne described this group as "storming" throughout
the semester! Without some sort of discussion—at least among the
three women—of how they wanted the group to proceed, each week's
meeting would begin anew the same pattern of clashing agendas, with
Frank trying to do the assignment he perceived, Anne trying to shut
Frank out of the group, Angie trying to bring him into the group, and
Sue staring at her desk, scared to speak.

For these students, group diversity was a problem at two levels. First, the very fact of diversity (of Frank's different ways of doing things, of their own different opinions) challenged them because of their conflicting expectations of how to talk to one another. Second, their lack of strategies for discussing these differences compounded these challenges, since the degree of diversity remained hidden from each of them most of the time. A process log from Angie during the last week of school illustrates the way this second item compounded the problem:

> I have a big problem I really couldn't discuss with the group. When we got together, Sue came up with feelings of the group's inability to gain anything from the experience. I realize she couldn't say much about anything in front of people, but her attitude really offended me. It was as though we had not tried. If she had shown me this goal instead of being negative and stubborn against Frank, maybe I would have had an easier time with it! The fact that we didn't perform completely as a group was known by all of us—something we had all written down. But I really have hard feelings since one of the major people who objected to Frank is saying that she couldn't get anything out of it—I really didn't witness much effort.

Angie, who'd struggled all semester to get the four to work together, reacts with private anger (expressed to her teacher, not to her group) when she finds out that Sue had shared her overall goals for group work but hadn't helped her improve the group—although Angie still can't blame Sue for not speaking openly about the conflicts in front of Frank. Clearly, diversity itself isn't the problem: it's the indirectness with which diversity is being confronted that leads to these private explosions of anger.

Even so, the group experience still proved useful for these people. In their end-of-the-semester portfolios, all of them identified ways in which they'd developed because of their group, from greater comfort in public speaking to a clearer sense of the many ways their writing affects people. And they did still feel themselves bonded as a group, even with all of the stress. Here's Anne, again:

> Since Frank joined our group, the three of us girls have had mixed emotions about him. Our communication with Frank has been all over. The four of us have clashing conversational assumptions.... [Yet] I am proud to say that Frank and I have started to become buds and I just try to overlook these things. Tuesday, when people were snickering about Frank's outside report, I was truly offended by these people. I think this is largely due to being in his small group all semester.... As small group members, it is easy to

become protective of one another due to the conversations that you have shared.

Even this group, troubled as it was, breeds a kind of group conscious-ness, a kind of gentle protectiveness, at the same time as it experiences anger and frustration. The same student who claimed all semester long to want to be in a group without Frank found herself wanting to defend him when others in class were making fun of him. Anne is perceptive enough to recognize that her protectiveness toward Frank stems from her group interaction with him at least as much as her frustration with him. She leaves the course stating that her group experience, while "stormy," has helped her understand her own and other's conversa-tional styles and helped her to improve her ability to get along with people significantly different than herself.

In sum, dealing with the diversity in small groups presents students with a variety of complex challenges and involves them in a variety of mixed emotions. How they are able to resolve these conflicts thus func-tions as a second enduring challenge in students' small-group experi-ence, equally as important as what to make of the interactions patterns they bring with them: Groups have people in them who are unlike you—what you do with these people will color your experience and in-fluence your learning.

Understanding Educational Contexts

A third enduring challenge for our students is what to make of the dif-ferences between writing classes that use small groups and other classes that do not. By the time our students come to us in college, they have had twelve or more years of schooling and have absorbed through these years a set of expectations about "how to do school," about the ways classes are run. When students find themselves in a writing class which emphasizes small-group work, especially when it's the first such class they've been in, they must work to make their own sense of the differences between this class and others.

A wonderful example of student work with these differences comes from Jennifer, a student in Rick's junior-level writing course for sec-ondary education majors. In her midsemester learning letter, Jennifer wrote:

> I guess I am not used to the really open system we have in this class. Actually, it frightens the hell out of me. I think my lack of fa-miliarity with [this] system . . . and my own personal pressures and insecurities combined have created a fear and discomfort.

She goes on to say:

> This sounds like I don't like the class or the system, but that is not so. On the contrary, it's been really good for me. . . . Overall, I feel more able to move in the direction that feels the best for the writer in me. I am doing more writing and feeling better about it.

Comments like Jennifer's are not unusual in writing classes at any level that use small groups. In fact, what she has to say captures very well part of what is happening to her and to students like her.

Most of Jennifer's previous writing classes were, in her terms, "closed" as opposed to "open." Her teachers told her what to write about, how to write it, and then indicated (generally in a sentence or two, followed by a grade) where she had succeeded or failed in following their directives. Writing had been a kind of demonstration, the sole purpose of which was to give those teachers what they wanted. On the other hand, in Rick's class, Jennifer had to decide for herself what she wanted to write about. She had to decide for herself how to write about it. And she received weekly responses to her writing, often when the writing was just beginning and was nowhere near ready for evaluation. Since those who most often responded to her writing were other members of her small group (people who found it uncomfortable to assume the traditional teacher's directive ways of reacting to writing), she could no longer be the traditional writing student. Writing could no longer be a demonstration. Instead, writing became a way of interacting with others, her written texts became things to share, and their purposes became purposes discovered in the interactive process of drafting and talking and drafting some more. As Jennifer so clearly describes it, the differences between her past educational experience and her small-group writing class are significant: an ongoing source of "fear and discomfort" as well as an ongoing opportunity "to move in the direction that feels best for the writer in me."

As "open" or "great for me" as her experience of writing and sharing her writing in her small group was, that experience was new. As "closed" or directive as her experience of writing in other classes had been, that experience was familiar. And the lure, the apparent safety of the familiar, was strong. In two different journals, we can begin to see something of the nature of Jennifer's struggle between what is safe but "closed," on the one hand, and what is risky but "open," on the other.

Very early in the semester, after the students had met a few times in their small groups, Rick told them he was interested in how their small groups were going, and that they might consider this a topic they could write to him about in their journals. Jennifer responded:

> As far as small groups go, I like the idea, but at the same time I feel
> like everybody is just trying to be nice. It kind of drives me crazy
> and I am guilty of it too. Maybe we should do [something where]
> each person talks about what they didn't like, didn't understand,
> thought was silly or unnecessary. I don't always want to hear
> what's good—not that I want to be burned at the stake . . . but it's
> hard for me to keep working on stuff when I've got an enormous
> buzz from my group digging what I write.

Until she entered Rick's class, Jennifer was familiar only with the ways
of responding to writing that she had experienced in her previous
"closed" writing classes. Usually the teachers pointed to what they
didn't like, didn't understand, thought was silly or unnecessary. And,
if Jennifer was allowed an opportunity to revise by changing these
points, she would. In Jennifer's past writing experience, the only possible reason for revision was that she had done something wrong. Now,
in her small group, her peers were instead pointing to what they liked,
what they understood or could relate to, and what they found interesting or engaging. Jennifer was familiar with how to respond to "decon-
structive criticism" (a phrase coined by one of the students in the class):
she would change what she had written to match her teacher's directives. However, when the responses of her peers were constructive
(new to her experience as a writer), she didn't know how to respond,
and it became hard for her "to keep working on stuff." She was confused and unsure of how she might use her peers' responses as she continued to write.

   This confusion helps explain the second journal entry, written in response to the class reading of Lucy Calkins's *Lessons from a Child* (1983).
Jennifer exhibited a very negative reaction to this book. The source of
this reaction, it seemed, appeared late in her journal: the success of
Suzie (the child of Calkins's title) as a writer terrified Jennifer. She
wrote:

> There are so many things I don't know. I feel like to be a great writ-
> ing teacher, you have to be a great writer. I am not. [T]he whole
> deal where Suzie is writing a million drafts of every line she
> [writes]. And, oh, what a good writer! I don't do that. I never have.
> Okay, maybe one or two rewrites but never over five. Come on. I
> guess I have a hard time looking at something I have just written
> and seeing ways to change and improve it. All the while I know the
> thing isn't perfect, but I just don't know how to go about changing
> it. What if the whole thing changes? I guess that's okay. I guess I
> could always change it back. I guess I need to practice. These are
> things I'm learning from this class. Wow. What a cool feeling.

At this point in the semester, Jennifer, a junior secondary education
major, was becoming aware that there is a connection between being a

writing teacher and being a writer. However, her only past under-standing of what it meant to be a writer came from her experiences in "closed" writing classes: writing for the teacher, either demonstrating or failing to demonstrate that she could follow teacher directives, and rewriting in order to make it right. Similarly, her only past under-standing of what it meant to be a writing teacher arose from the same experiences. Calkins's Suzie, the fourth-grade girl who exploded into writing when given charge over her own topics, writing tempos, and response, offered Jennifer another model of a writer: a writer who writes "a million" drafts, writes to understand and to share what she understands with others, a writer who owns her experience of doing writing. *Of course* Jennifer was terrified. What if someday she had a stu-dent like Suzie in her classroom? What if she had a student who was a "really great writer," perhaps a better writer than Jennifer herself? How could she then be the sort of writing teacher she had experienced?

As the semester progressed, Jennifer responded by trying to become more like the sort of writer she was experiencing in her small group, the sort of writer Suzie represented. In another journal entry, she wrote of her semester's experience in her small group:

> I began writing. I could do what I wanted when I wanted and that's it. I could share what I wanted. Everything I did, I did on my own and because I wanted to. The end result was something that was great for me: I did more writing than I ever have. And it was good.

Jennifer's discovery of an alternative model for being a writer and for doing what a writer does (and, subsequently, for being a writing teacher and doing what a writing teacher does) was very significant. During an early semester visit in Rick's office, Jennifer told him that "obviously" she was not "a great writer" or even "a good writer." Ac-tually, she said that she didn't really think of herself as "a writer at all." She certainly didn't much like to write. These feelings toward writing stemmed from her understanding of writing as that understanding was formed in her previous educational experience, in the classes she would refer to as "closed" in her journal. However, recall that in her midsemester learning letter, Jennifer begins to assume responsibility for and control over her writing experience, and the result is that she writes more and believes it is "good." Clearly, within this new and dif-ferent—"open"—educational context, Jennifer comes to understand that she is a writer—or at least that she is in touch with that "writer in me." She writes in another journal entry: "I have always wanted to write. It's in me, I know it is. It makes me happy."

Jennifer's discovery was neither easy for her nor ever really com-plete. Once again, in her learning letter, she writes:

> I think a good way to describe the nature of my experience as a
> writer would be to describe to you what went into this letter. I have
> been thinking for a while what I would write. Thinking about the
> things I wanted you to know. I've tried to sit down and actually do
> the writing 2 or 3 times before this one. Well, it's 9 in the morning
> on the day this is to be handed in and I am finally doing it. I get
> myself all worked up. I want my writing to be fantastic, clear, in-
> teresting, exactly what I want the first time I write it. Once I get
> going I don't necessarily feel that way anymore. I've tried to figure
> out the reason for this in the past few days. I put a lot of pressure
> on myself to be a "good" writer (whatever that is), to be a "serious"
> writer (whatever that is). I think it is probably the outcome of a few
> scattered but humiliating experiences where my words were con-
> sidered less than acceptable.

Still, she writes:

> Things are happening for me [as a writer] and I think it's because
> I am finally being given the opportunity to let them happen.

Jennifer continues to find it difficult to be a writer different from the
kind of writer she learned to be in her "closed" writing classrooms.
However, she knows "things are happening." She is writing more. She
enjoys her writing experience. She believes that what she has finished
is good. Jennifer, in short, is wrestling productively with the differences
between her past educational experience and the experience of her
small-group-based writing class. She feels fear, discomfort, and growth,
and much of her journal writing is an attempt to put into words and
hence understand these competing feelings. In her journals, she is more
articulate than many of our students about the tensions she feels about
her clashing educational experiences, but even so, her words document
a common feeling for many students when they begin to share writing
in small groups. One of the greatest powers of small groups is to provide students with an alternative educational context within which to
be a writer and explore what a writer does—but this great power is also
a source of significant discomfort because it makes the writing class different from most other school experiences.

Conclusion

In this chapter, we've tried to present some of the ways our students
experience their small response groups and some of the major challenges they face as they interact. The challenges are often located in differences: differences between private issues they want to write about
and the public discussion of opinions (and other "private" matters) in

college classes; differences between individuals who come from diverse geographic, ethnic, and political backgrounds; and differences between this school context and others. In our talks with teachers at national conventions, in first-year writing courses on up to graduate writing workshops, these same three challenges arise consistently. As teachers interested in using small groups, in helping students to deal with the plurality and difference that characterize small groups and the wider culture in which we all live, we feel a responsibility to name these challenges and to ponder strategies that can help students negotiate them successfully.

Note

1. She borrowed the word "storming" from the traditional description of group development through stages—*storming, norming,* and *performing*—which Robert had presented in class as an aid for reflection. According to the literature on group theory (Tuckman 1965; Rothwell 1992), the *storming* stage is characterized by clashes of individual agendas, as the group struggles to work out for itself a set of regular procedures and roles for its members; the *norming* stage occurs as the group moves out of storming into the establishment of standard procedures and roles; and the *performing* stage occurs once the norms have been established and the group falls into a pattern of performing according to the procedures and roles it has created. Group theory claims that all groups have to move through these stages to function and that the negotiations are internal to the group even when an external purpose is assigned the group from an outside authority. Anne felt that her group hadn't achieved a norming stage because collectively they couldn't decide how to deal with the differences in their group.

3 Teaching from Experience, Claiming Small Groups

Robert Brooke
University of Nebraska–Lincoln

Ruth Mirtz
Florida State University

Rick Evans
University of Nebraska–Lincoln

It's a late October Monday morning in Nebraska, and it snowed the night before. I come into the mail room about 8:20, still unraveling the scarf I've just today pulled from the cedar storage chest, and there's Ruth, already here, talking to Karen, one of the new teaching assistants who pulled the dreaded 7:30 class duty. They're talking about small groups in Karen's class, and I listen in.

"They warned me to expect *one* dysfunctional group," Karen jokes, "but I have a *whole class* that's dysfunctional!"

She proceeds to tell us about a young man who won't point out what's good in his colleague's writing, but instead responds only with wisecracks. "They think he's funny," she says, exasperated, "but he also stops them from talking about the pieces because they're scared of his wit. I've told him we appreciate his wisecracks but we need to know what he likes, too, and he just rolls his eyes."

Ruth listens supportively and tells a story about a student in her class a few years back who started skipping small-group days and turning in papers only to her, and how frustrating that is for us who believe that learning is cooperative. . . .

It's noon hour, and I come up from my office to play cribbage over lunch, only to find Rick talking to Margrethe and Joy, blocking the doorway. They're talking about small groups in Margrethe's classes—she's just up from a small-group session that went *wonderfully,* she says. She tells us how while she was modeling the group response procedures by having her students respond to something she wrote overnight, one of the students said he thought she cherished writing. "Wonderful!" she says. "And it came from *him,* not *me.* I think we're really getting somewhere." Rick agrees and follows up with a story of one of his classes at Texas A&M, about how clear it is to him that learning works best when students themselves initiate it. Joy complicates matters with another story of a student in her advanced writing class who disagreed with an insight another student had—maybe, she thinks aloud, what works for one student impedes others, so to sponsor diversity effectively, we really need to allow each student to find her own way? . . .

It's late afternoon and the sun is setting behind the trees outside the mailroom window. The fading light does something strange to the institutional greys of the mailboxes, the institutional blues of the walls, and the anti-institutional reds and purples of Judy's and Susan's parkas. When I come in, they're discussing the differences between small groups in Composition 150 and Fiction Writing 254. Judy finds her students are responding better in their journals than in the small groups themselves, and she wonders about differences between private dialogues with her as trusted adult versus the riskier public dialogue of the small group. Susan finds the criminal justice majors a source of stress in her fiction workshop because they seem to just *like* everything and aren't as critical of the clichéd stories as she wishes they were. As Judy and Susan talk, they wonder if their own experience working in groups doesn't highlight these features for them. Judy tells about her writing group in Omaha, and Susan tells about her years of experience in creative writing workshops.

—Excerpt from Robert Brooke's
teaching journal

If small groups confront students with challenges based on differences, small groups also present teachers with challenges. Where students worry about voicing their private concerns in the public arena of groups, about people who are different from themselves, and about the educational context itself, teachers have their own list of worries. In addition to worrying about individual differences or whether or not to write about personal material, teachers tell us they ask themselves questions like these: "How can I maintain control over what happens in small groups, when there are eight groups and I'm only one person?" "How can I ensure that the comments they make to each other are valid, useful, and connected to what the writer needs?" "How do I manage groups that are silent, that don't seem to work well together— or, on the other hand, groups that are too talkative, talking about everything but the writing?" "What will I be sacrificing that I can do through whole-class interaction or through individual conferences, if I allot my class time to small groups instead of these matters?"

On the surface, many of these questions seem to be about classroom management, about how to conduct the activities of class in such a way that they succeed. They are questions about our own actions as teachers, posed from a way of thinking about teaching which we have all inherited: we imagine the teacher as that controlling figure standing at the front of the classroom, monitoring all the interaction that goes on, responsible for guiding the discourse of the classroom through the time-honored rituals of lecturing, Socratic questioning, and the calling for raised hands to let only one student speak at a time. When we think of the role of the teacher in American education, it's images like these which we imagine. They're what we experienced when we went to school; they're what the media presents whenever sit-coms or movies show classrooms, from "Welcome Back, Kotter" to *Stand and Deliver* to *The Corn Is Green*. In our culture, the role of the teacher is that of a controlling presence in the classroom, controlling discourse and controlling behavior. Most of the questions that spring immediately to mind about small groups originate from the presence of this image in the back of teachers' minds. Most of these questions, in fact, stem from one central question, one only rarely articulated: "If I put my students in small groups, how on earth will I maintain control over them?"

In this chapter, we want to suggest that we can't think about small groups productively as long as we ask only this question (or its derivatives). The fact of the matter is that you can't control what goes on in small groups. No matter how rigidly you structure their discussion through handouts and assigned roles and required reports, the small group creates an educational setting where you are present only in absentia, and where the students themselves must negotiate among themselves what their own agendas are and the degree to which they will pay attention to what you, as teacher, have required of them. If you choose to use small groups in your classroom, you are making a choice to give up, at least partially, some of the control over classroom discourse and behavior that traditional teaching involves. For any teacher who thinks of teaching only through our culture's standard images of teaching, small groups can only pose a threat.

We believe that small groups connect more strongly with a different role we take on as professional educators: the role of writer. While we acknowledge that small-group pedagogy always challenges to some degree the traditional role of all-controlling teacher, we believe that small groups allow your role as writer to come out more strongly and more forcefully in the classroom. Small groups create many of the same situations through which we each learned to value writing: they surround growing writers with a social purpose for writing, with lively conversation about things they've written, and with other people who write, some more effectively and some less effectively than they do. Using small groups in the writing classroom can allow the role of writer to become more central and more important for all concerned, teacher as well as students, than the traditional educational roles of controller and controlled, guide and learner, that exist in most other classroom environments.

In this chapter, we would like to share some stories of how small groups have connected with our own growing experience as writers. We offer these stories largely to highlight the ways small-group pedagogy has resonated with parts of our experience other than our traditional teacher's role. For each of us as writers, we found we could look back on our lives and identify crucial groups that had supported us in becoming the kind of writers we are today, from Robert's own experience with informal and special-purpose writing groups, to Rick's work with the Iowa Writing Lab, to Ruth's family and church experiences. For each of us, the ways in which we structure our writing classes and in which we use small groups within those classes derive finally from these past experiences, from a motivated attempt to recreate with our students some of the contexts in which we ourselves learned to value writing as an important act in our own lives.

To use small groups in writing classes, we expect, requires teachers to engage in a similar kind of search, a search for the contexts in which they themselves emerged as writers and for the groups that supported them. We offer these personal stories, in short, as vicarious experiences through which you might begin to search your own past. As Kathy Carter (1993) has argued recently, "A story, in other words, is a theory of something. What we tell and how we tell it is a revelation of what we believe. . . . Through story, teachers transform knowledge . . . into a form that plays itself out in the time and space of classrooms" (7–9). We offer these stories as a theory of how we came to see small groups as important in our pedagogy. In the chapters that make up part II of this book, we will describe the time and space of the classrooms that these stories inform.

Robert's Story: Small Groups as a Way of Being

I've been using small groups as part of my composition classes since I began teaching in 1979 at the University of Minnesota. Day one of their teacher-training seminar: a forty-minute writing on an event important to us, and then we were in small groups. I remember that group: Dexter, our group leader for the day, asking us to read our pieces aloud (Dex would later become my office mate); Paula, an intense Episcopalian from Chicago, responding with support and pleasure to other's writing but timidly hiding her own (she too would become a friend during graduate school); Bill, a big man with a beard who had started an art critique of the current Walker Center show (he'd later work with Kate, my spouse, in a course for writing in the arts). I remember the talk about the origin of our ideas, about whether we'd written on them before, about how we thought we normally acted as writers. This experience was supposed to introduce us to ways in which we could use small groups in our own writing classes. Later, in about week eight of the seminar, we would read Peter Elbow's *Writing without Teachers* (1973) and a summary of Ernest Bormann's task/maintenance functions (1975; 1990) and argue about the ways our students were acting in groups, but for that moment, as a new teacher in my first teacher-training seminar, I found myself feeling relieved and encouraged. I'd been worried about how "they" would ask me to teach (in fact, I hadn't slept the night before), but writing groups were something I knew about, something I knew how to do.

Looking back on that experience from the benefit of eleven years' teaching, I can now see why I'd felt immediately comfortable: my past life as a writer, organizing and working with creative writing groups in high school and college, had already prepared me to believe that group interaction is central to a writer's development. But this self-knowledge is a later theory, something I've come to through struggle with good classes and bad, through an intellectual shift that allows me to bridge my early experience with creative writing with my adult experience with academic writing. At the time, all I had was a felt sense that this would be a "do-able" way of teaching, not the drill and lecture that I'd worried I'd be asked to do. Small groups felt right in the writing classroom because I'd already had lots of experience with them. As a pedagogic device, they plugged into things I knew. Although I couldn't put this connection into words when I started teaching, I'm sure that my immediate comfort with groups in writing classes grew out of my experience with that way of being a writer.

Ever since I first began writing, what's provided me with the impetus for writing has been groups of other writers with whom I shared my work. It's been in that context that my writing has always developed: in every new job or college or school I've been in since high school, I've either plugged into existing writing groups or formed them when they were not yet present. It's never been enough just to have other people read and respond to my work (though that's been important); I've personally needed to surround myself with other writers writing, to read their work as they read mine, and to explore writing together.

When I reconstruct my life with this idea in mind, I realize that, for me this experience of writing in the presence of others started in second grade. Miss Clausen, my teacher at Graland Country Day School in Denver, set up her second-grade classroom in a way that must have been a precursor to the elementary writing workshops we now associate with Lucy Calkins (1986) and Donald Graves (1984). She'd give us story starters, and we'd write for a while, and then we'd put away our half-finished drafts and talk with each other about our ideas, before coming back to our writings the next day and adding to the stories. I remember writing a long epic story late in second grade about four anthropomorphized insects who went on a journey into the house of the human beings. Every day, I'd develop the characters of the grasshopper, the fly, the beetle, and the lady bug a little more, and write them into incredible cliff-hangers: about to be squished by the boys' pillow fighting, sucked up into the vacuum cleaner and trapped inside the dusty bag, etc. I never knew how to get them out of these dilemmas, and so I'd stop, stumped, until after recess. You see, during recess (and the time just before, when Miss Clausen would have us talk to each other) I'd tell my friends Dan and Andrew about my story, and they'd give me ideas about what might happen (Dan usually had good ideas involving what I'd later come to know as deus ex machina solutions; Andrew would usually tell me what would happen if I didn't get my bugs out of the mess, enjoying the "Calvin and Hobbes" details of bug's innards and separated body parts). And they'd tell me about their stories, and I'd give my suggestions. I honestly don't remember what Miss Clausen ever did with those stories or if I ever finished them—what I do remember was the pace of the writing: writing, talking, then writing some more, in continual dialogue with others who were also doing these things.

Miss Clausen's class, I now realize, was unusual for that time in American education, and I certainly never experienced its like again until reading about the elementary classrooms in Calkins's *Lessons from a Child*. But in retrospect, I can see myself starting as a writer there.

If I jump ahead to junior high school, over four or five years of not writing much at all, I see a resurgence of writing at a time when once again I was surrounded by a writer's group. Mrs. Bisby, the seventh- and ninth-grade English teacher, organized each year the Graland literary magazine, and she asked Dan and me to join the staff in seventh grade. It was one of the big choices in my life—the literary magazine staff met the same hour as band, so I had to choose between playing tuba and writing. Looking back on that time, I think I liked music more than writing and, if I'd known myself better, might have preferred band. But, as a straggly seventh grader, smaller than the other boys, long on imagination and short on charm, I chose the literary magazine staff because it would mean more social time. Dan would be there, and the staff talked a lot; in band, all you did was play.

What I found when I joined the group was the same sort of experience I'd had in second grade. Each meeting, we'd read through the submissions the magazine had received that week (from seventh through ninth graders), and we'd discuss the pieces and suggest revisions, rejections, or publication. Often, the writers of the pieces were in the room—usually at least one staff member brought in a piece he or she had written—and so the talk was both about our reactions as readers and about the writer's own feelings about the text. (I don't remember whether or not Mrs. Bisby guided these discussions, but I rather expect she did—she was an authoritative, organized, no-nonsense person.) It took me a total of two meetings before I got the bug and started writing myself, and over the course of the next three years, I wrote a host of poems and six short stories which I shared in the context of that group. The readings and discussion gave me a chance to shine before my peers in ways I couldn't elsewhere. During recess or in gym, I was awkward and shy and was treated that way, but during literary magazine meetings people would listen to what I had to say. Although the pressures of junior high social interaction were strong enough that members of the staff didn't really interact outside of meetings (we all kept to our social groups, such as they were), for that period each week, we shared a care for writers and writing. I think I learned then that anyone, no matter what that person's other roles were, could be a writer (the staff ranged across all the junior high groups—an athlete, two of the "popular" girls, a boy destined to be class president, and several of us seeming maladapts). Through staff discussions and Mrs. Bisby's resources, we provided each other with a good deal of support for writing and encouraged each other to take our work seriously enough to submit it to national and adolescent magazines. By the end of ninth grade, each of us had collected at least one rejection slip.

Throughout adolescence, I think I knew in some corner of my being that I needed the group to continue writing. I was not doing well in school itself—the endless grammar drills and five-paragraph essay exams didn't hold much juice for me—but I really enjoyed the reading and writing I did outside of school. With Dan and the staff, I could talk about what I was reading, and they'd probably read it too or suggest other things like it. With Dan and the staff, I'd share ideas for stories, and pretty soon all of us would be writing detective stories or horror stories; I could hardly wait to get to study hall so we could pass our stories back and forth to read them. But I noticed about myself that, over the summer, when we didn't see each other and only my mother and father and rest of the family were around, I'd slowly stop writing. Other things would take over—football at Seventh Avenue parkway, basketball in the church playground, or just watching "The Avengers" reruns on Channel 12 until late at night. I enjoyed doing these other things, but I also felt like I was letting myself down. Every spring during junior high, I'd leave for the summer full of plans for stories to write before the fall started up again, sure I'd impress Dan and the staff and Mrs. Bisby when I returned; but every fall would come and the stories would still be airy fancies lacking local habitation and a name.

I think it's because of this felt need for a writing group that when I went on to East High in Denver, I formed my own writing group. I needed to because the sources of group support I'd had before crumbled. Dan had gone east to boarding school. The Denver high schools did publish a literary magazine, but it was unreachable since it was competitive and published stuff from *all* the Denver high schools. The staff were only seniors and were elected or appointed and met once a month at Thomas Jefferson High. So, as a sophomore, I couldn't be on that staff, and since we were only doing essays and book reports in my English classes, I found myself needing to form a group outside of school.

At first, I started by asking people who impressed me at school to form a writer's club with me, and even though many of the ones I asked didn't initially consider themselves writers, most agreed. At that age, I don't think I had a clue as to who I was looking for when I asked people—I chose folks on the basis of whether or not I liked them. I remember asking Dave and Ben, two brothers in my American history class, largely because they seemed so clever in class discussion—I was sure they'd be interested. (Months later, Dave's girlfriend told me that he had been frightened when I first approached him because he saw himself as good in math but not in English and because he had always gotten help on his class essays.) Looking back, I suppose what I was offering these people wasn't to their minds a writing group, but friendship, a chance to join something, to be young intellectuals. Maybe it was that which they responded to.

I remember the first night we met—a semiformal occasion in my parents' living room. There were seven of us there: me, the two brothers, their friend Tobin from another high school, Linda (who I'd known at Graland), Kim (a musician from American history class), and Robin (a woman who had overheard me ask Ben and volunteered her own interest). We were all a little tense. I had a story with me and I think we began with it, establishing out of ignorance a pattern we'd later follow: I read the piece aloud, then, scared by the awkward silence when no one said anything, I told them what I'd been thinking about when I wrote the piece and tried to protect myself by telling them what I thought still needed work in it. Soon they started responding to what I'd said—Tobin had advice about the trouble spots, Robin was interested in what I'd been thinking, Ben had read something like it and told us about that. As the conversation died down, it turned out that Tobin had brought some of his poetry along, and so he read that, told us about the poems, and we talked. By now it was getting late, and so Robin asked if we could meet next week at her house and she'd have a story for us. We were off and running. In the weeks that followed, everyone but Kim brought something they'd written; all of us invited friends we knew to join us, and the meetings flourished, ranging on any given night from five to fourteen people in attendance and from one to four people sharing work.

By the end of my sophomore year, this writing group was a well-established part of the East High adolescent scene. We chose to keep meeting over the summer, and did. We started hanging out together, dating each other, going to music shows together as well as meeting for writing, so I suppose the idea of the group offering friendship was at least as important as the writing. But it was actually more complex than that—some people only showed up for writing group meetings, and a lot of other people went to music shows with us, so I suspect friendship and writing were intertwined amidst all the other thoughts and feelings we had as teenagers.

By the time I left East High several years later, this informal group had become institutionalized as one of East High's clubs. We had a faculty sponsor and a way of recruiting new members through the English teachers, and we had a membership of around thirty people. I wrote a great deal for this group (more, in fact, than I was being asked to write in school), and I still have in my basement the drafts I wrote then: hundred-page beginnings of two fantasy novels, a collection of horror stories, a number of love poems, some song lyrics—the assorted embarrassing shards of one writer's beginnings. I continued to submit my work to magazines and continued to collect rejection slips, though several of my colleagues were successful in their submissions. Two of the women in the group landed scholarships to major Eastern colleges, largely on the basis of their potential in creative writing. Once again, the group provided a necessary context for my writing, although by this point in my life, I had somehow known to create this context for myself when my school would not offer it.

The same story occurred in college, at Gonzaga University. I started a writers' group with interested English majors in my courses; we began meeting once a week for discussion and pizza; by the time I left GU, this group had become institutionalized with faculty advisors and recruitment procedures. It kept me writing; in my senior year, I won Gonzaga's Costello Poetry Award with attendant rights to publish the poem in that year's literary magazine—my first and only published creative piece in some seven years of trying.

But something else happened during those college years: I began to focus on critical writing as well as on creative writing. At Gonzaga, the writers' group was a creative writing group, sharing poetry and fiction primarily, but an informal critical writing group also existed. In good Jesuit tradition, all our humanities teachers assigned papers every five weeks, so my friends and I found ourselves writing often for philosophy, history, social science, and English classes. We didn't think of this writing as anything more than assigned writing, but as I look back on it, we surrounded these critical papers with as much informal discussion as we gave our creative writing in writers' group meetings.

Following traditional student practice, we all wrote the final drafts of our papers the night before they were due (a few of us wrote drafts earlier, but not many). After classes were over for the day, I'd return to my dorm room and start banging out a draft on my Olympia portable, and my classmates would go off to their dorms, apartments, or the library to work on their papers. About ten or eleven at night, we'd all find ourselves at Pakie's, the all-night greasy spoon a few blocks from campus, reading each other's papers over "Student Stuffers," coffee, and soft-serve ice cream. On any given night, our informal group would include several of us working on the same paper assignment as well as several other people (like my roommate John, the math major) who just liked the discussions. We'd read and react to these papers, both by discussing the content and by discussing the professors we were writing them for, and then about midnight or 1 a.m. we'd all return to where we'd come from to type out the revised, final drafts that had emerged from these discussions.

At the time, I didn't claim this informal process of sharing critical writing as a response group (just as, in second grade and junior high, I hadn't understood my creative writing groups as response groups). But looking back, I can see myself developing in those Pakie's all-nighters a sense of response as a necessary stage in critical writing as well as creative writing. And during college the critical writing became more important for me. When I applied to graduate schools, I applied as an English major, not a creative writer. Though I still wrote poetry and fiction on the side, I had become interested enough in literary history and theory to want to pursue those areas in graduate school. I moved to

Minnesota, expecting to specialize in medieval studies, hoping to develop my abilities to write the types of essays written by academics in departments of English.

At Minnesota, I began writing my academic papers in solitude and didn't join the existing circle of creative writers. But by the end of my third year (by which time I'd decided to specialize in composition), I had made the connection with my undergraduate experience and saw the need for the same kind of writing group for academic writing as I'd had earlier for creative writing. So, under the pressure of needing other minds to respond to my attempts at articles and my dissertation, I pushed the program to start what would become Minnesota's Composition Colloquium, where writers from the area bring in drafts-in-process and get response toward publication. That group followed functionally the same patterns my earlier creative writing groups had followed, although now the texts being responded to were academic rather than creative. At Minnesota, I found the Colloquium invaluable in keeping me writing, probably because it provided the kind of writer's community I'd grown to expect.

I haven't laid out this progression for myself before on paper, but here it is. Looking at it, I can see several things, all of which are important: for me, writing only remained important if I was surrounded with groups of other writers, also writing; for my own development as a writer, it didn't matter that my work was less successful than the work of my peers, or that we sometimes had negative things to say about each other's work—what did matter was that we shared the activity of writing and at least held a common value or interest in writing as being worthwhile; the group support worked as well for academic writing as for creative writing; and, finally, throughout my experience with writing groups, the social side of group interaction has been as important as the writing itself.

I grew as a writer by interacting with other writers. The possibility of being part of a writer's community helped me find a way of being in the world during my early and late adolescent years, providing me with a sense that I could share some interests and activities with others my age, even though I wasn't an athlete or a particularly good student or a charmer at the awkward dances. As I've matured, I've retained this early lesson about writing groups as a sort of root experience with which I approach the world: writing is an exciting and interesting activity that can help you connect to people, form friendships and social networks, and produce work that can influence your world.

When, in that first teaching seminar at Minnesota, I breathed a sigh of relief because I was being asked to make small groups part of my composition pedagogy, I think that sense of relief was borne of this root experience. The way I'd been living, in my writing and my social life, flowed through the dynamics of writing groups. I was in familiar territory and would be able to find my feet as a teacher of composition.

Rick's Story: Writing as a Way of Participating

Relative to other academics, I suspect that I was very late coming to an understanding of myself as a writer, as someone with something important to say to someone else. Throughout my years of schooling, I thought of myself (had only been allowed to think of myself) as someone trying and failing to be a "good writer." I learned to avoid writing. I was convinced that I could not write and that I would never become a good writer. The world of words and how to use them properly was not mine. I was a child in the sense described by Simone de Beauvoir in "Personal Freedom and Others" (1980). I was unaware not only of myself, but of myself as an essential participant in the world around me. As long as I could avoid the world—and writing as a way of participating in that world—I remained "happily irresponsible."

Then, during the final semester of my senior year in college, a graduate student friend of mine suggested that I enroll in a class called "Literature and Culture of Twentieth-Century America." I had taken a few English classes (only those with multiple-choice or maybe essay exams) and liked the reading. My friend also told me that the instructor did not require papers; instead, he asked for something called a reading journal. Each journal need only be a page long, he claimed, and students could write about anything they wanted. Of course, I was skeptical. However, my friend had been so enthusiastic (besides I didn't need the credits to graduate, so I could drop) that I agreed to do the class the first day and check it out.

The class began in an unusual way. The instructor told us how demanding the semester would be and that feeling this demand was an important way of gauging our own involvement with what we were learning—no instructor had ever talked before about whether or not I should be involved in learning. He passed out a description of the reading journal, and I read it very carefully. At the head of the handout were these epigraph-like sayings:

> Why not speak for yourself
> Sooner or later you'll have to.

> [and]

If you want to use somebody's else's ruler
[to measure your life], that's your business.

In what followed, I thought I heard someone asking, challenging me to speak for myself, to say what I thought, not what I thought someone else wanted to hear. I had never before heard anyone talk about writing, or writing in response to reading, in this way. The next day I registered for the class.

The first journal entry was due the last day of September, too late for me to drop the class, and I was frightened. What if, I thought, when someone asked me to speak for myself, I had nothing to say? I wrote about Dreiser's novel *Sister Carrie.* I wrote and rewrote and rewrote that entry and, in order to ensure a positive response, I made it four pages. I even handed it in a day late, reading the words over and over again, long after I was able to hear what they were saying. The instructor told us that the grade didn't count—it was just a sign to let us know that we were heading in the right direction. It mattered to me, however—it was an "F." "I don't want a plot summary," he wrote. The very next day I was in his office and finally admitted to someone else what I had known for quite some time. "I can't write," I said, "I just can't."

We talked for maybe an hour or so, and to his credit he realized that he was not about to convince me otherwise. I offered him an alternative. If I talked into a tape recorder and periodically handed in the tapes and the recorder, would he listen, evaluate me this way? He didn't like my alternative much, but as his purpose, he reminded me, was to teach, not evaluate, he agreed. Immediately, I was off to buy a tape recorder and with it a renewed sense of self-confidence.

I had always been a good talker or so I thought until I started talking into the microphone about Stein's *Three Lives*. I began to realize how much understanding my listeners gave me. It seemed unnatural to speak without the responsive gestures of someone else's face or the reshaping echo of another's voice. I found myself trying with singularly profound punch lines to say all that could be said about Melanchta's consumption and its relation to American culture. Or, I babbled, filling a half-hour tape with empty generalizations that seemed to stumble over one another in a kind of silly-sounding slapstick. The point is that both comedic routines were just that. And, the next entry was due the middle of October.

Once more I sat down with pencil and paper, resigning myself to predictable failure rather than risking anything new and possibly final. I had a response to *Three Lives:* Stein destroyed Melanchta Herbert. So with that response, I began my entry. I wrote about how Melanctha had always been set up: "Always Melanctha Herbert had wanted peace and quiet, and always she could not find ways to get excited . . . new ways to be in trouble." I felt sorry for Melanctha, yet I knew why Stein had destroyed her: "Stein, through her destruction of Melanctha, points to the need for . . . the creative power of a personality that can live within chaos, with uncertainty." I was careful to make my case, and then I forgot my case, at least as much as I was able: "How many conflicts do we really have within ourselves? . . . It's no wonder mankind reaches desperately for God," I wrote, "who else could understand our complexity?" "C-" was his grade that didn't count. He wrote underneath, "You're raising important and relevant questions, but not taking them personally. How do these questions relate to your own life, and do you have any answers?"

It was the minus that bothered me. I was revealing myself more in this journal entry than in anything I had ever written before. The next day I returned to his office and told him that he had misread my entry. I told him that those questions were personal. They were questions I was struggling with at that very moment in trying to plan my future after college. It was the first time I had ever argued for something I had written. It was the first time I had ever cared to. I told him that I thought I deserved a "B." To my surprise, he agreed, and I discovered, however superficially, what Simone de Beauvoir suggests that a child discovers as he moves into adolescence: "He discovers his own subjectivity [and] he discovers the subjectivity of others. . . . " Soon I became a regular visitor during his office hours. We would at least begin by talking about what I had read, but the talk inevitably wandered to other things. Sometimes we would even talk about what he had written. Even though many of his articles and books were beyond my understanding, I still enjoyed reading the writing of someone I knew. Mostly, however, we told stories, and we became friends-for-a-semester.

Now, as I look back on that time, I feel that he must have seen in my desperate protest and in my many visits to his office that I was trying, trying to move beyond my childhood and those routines that protected and prevented me from engaging the life that is literature with the life of my own self. The point was not simply to reveal myself, but to find in the expression of self a way of participating in and assuming responsibility for my own view of the world, something I had always before (at least in a school context) considered inappropriate.

The third journal entry was to be the last sample before turning in the completed journal on the last day of class. It was due the middle of November. At the time I was reading and rereading *The Education of Henry Adams*, and for a while ignoring the long list of other books (twenty or more as I remember). I was drawn to the chapter entitled

"Chaos," and to Adams's own description of his response to the death of his sister. Adams writes that

> [he] had been some three weeks in London when he received a telegram from his brother-in-law . . . telling him that his sister had been thrown from a cab and injured, and that he had better come . . . Tetanus had already set in . . .

He said of the experience that followed that

> the last lesson, sum and term of education, began then. He had passed through thirty years of rather varied experience without once having the shell of custom broken. He had never seen Nature, only her surface, the sugar-coating that she shows youth. Flung suddenly in his face, with the harsh brutality of chance . . . he found his sister, a woman of forty, as gay and brilliant in the terrors of lockjaw as she had been in careless fun . . . lying in bed as a consequence of a miserable cab accident that had bruised her foot. Hour by hour [her] muscles grew rigid, while [her] mind remained bright, until after ten days of fiendish torture she died in convulsions.

And I remembered the death of my own sister.

For fifteen years I had been an only child, living with the smiling attention and the frightened sense of obligation that all only-children feel. I wanted a sister, someone else my parents could love and someone who, as an older brother, I could love, too. On the twelfth of August my mother carried Lisa Diane through the front door of our house and into my life. She was not quite two weeks old and adopted. That made her even more special. "Our little present," my mother called her.

Lisa's first months with us must have been exhausting for her. Whenever she was not sleeping, and sometimes even if she was, I was either feeding, talking, playing, or all of these at once with her. I learned to listen at night through the bedroom wall for the slightest whimper, and then race my mother to warm the milk. "First up, right to feed" was the rule. Once she had been fed and was awake, the fun would begin. I would hold her upright in my lap, wanting her hands to grab at my nose, pull my hair. I suppose it's because babies are trying to learn what to look at when people talk to them, but Lisa seemed to be looking at the whole of my face, never at any one part. Her deep brown eyes seemed to grow larger in order to include all of me. She would smile then as if to tell me that she enjoyed my silliness. I loved that she only knew me as a wonderful whole of colors and contours. I felt at ease with her.

One evening during her first Christmas time, Lisa and I were again in our favorite chair watching each other. Our parents were gone to one of those Christmas parties. We were alone together. We were talking of Santa Claus when her eyes began to flutter, jerk up and back. Her head pulled away from me. First her neck then her back tightened into a unnatural arch. Her arms grew stiff. Her legs straightened.

I tried to talk with her. "Lisa, what's wrong?" I said. "Are you all right?" I held her close to me, trying firmly but gently to flatten her neck and back again. "Lisa," I shouted. I was scared. I held her away from me. Helpless. "Lisa," I said, "it's me," almost as if she were then supposed to comfort me. I brought her close to me again, stood up, and started to walk back and forth across the room. "Lisa," I whispered into her ear. Then, as quickly as she had changed, she changed again. Her muscles relaxed, her body softened, her eyes grew dark and inclusive like before. Lisa died two months later as a result of surgery to repair a birth defect.

I wrote of Lisa in that third entry and of her death. I began, "Henry Adams calls the death of his sister the last lesson, the sum and term of his education." I asked a question: "What does it mean to know death?" My answer at the end of the entry was that "I can only know life. What I'm trying to say is that death can only be known as it reflects life, or rather what of life we have lost. What of life Adams lost was his sister and with her his belief in order, purpose, and reason. What I had known of life was my sister Lisa. What I learned of death was life without her." At the bottom of the last page my reader/teacher wrote "Thank you" and an "A."

In the month and one-half that remained of the semester, I wrote nearly one hundred pages in response to the readings. I had begun to understand writing as a way of speaking for myself and reading as a way of listening to others speak for themselves. As a writer and as a person, I had grown. Through a very special relationship that surrounded writing with real person-to-person talk—rather than teacher-to-student or student-to-teacher talk and that demanded self-involvement in personal and sometimes even painful ways—I discovered that I was free, free to make myself a presence in the world, free as well to engage in the awful responsibility of revealing myself and responding to the selves that others revealed. I was no longer the child I had been. I knew I was learning. Yet, without a particular reader's continued and constant willingness to begin with me in my writing (and often with my own misunderstandings), I might never have understood that I could learn from myself in my writing and from the selves that others shared with me in their writing.

I replaced my need to be a good writer with a need to write, to have others read and respond to what I had written, and to read the writing

of others. Writing became a way of acting and interacting, a way of participating with my own learning and in the learning of others. However, as is often the case with students, once that special reader/teacher
relationship ended with the semester, I was alone, again. There were no
others to read and respond. There were no others whose writing I could
read. There were no opportunities to talk about writing or what had
been written. I felt as if this particular teacher had given me a great gift,
but that now there were no more chances for me to use this gift or to
share it with others. My response was to apply to graduate school in
English. I hoped that other English teachers might become my readers,
too. But that didn't happen. They again wanted me to be a good writer,
without allowing me to act as a writer and to interact with other writers. I struggled. Of course, I found ways to force those teachers to respond, to talk about my writing. Yet my experiences as a writer, as a
reader, and as a learner were never as positive, powerful, or productive
as before. I continued to search. I wanted and needed more than a single responsive and responsible teacher. I wanted and needed a community of writers. It wasn't until I volunteered to teach in the
University of Iowa Writing Lab that I found such a community, a dynamic community of students and teachers all writing, and all talking
about writing.

The Lab I entered was a different sort of place. It was at least three
to four times larger than a normal classroom, with big round tables instead of desks, carefully placed in the open spaces throughout the
room. Paintings announced themselves on the wall, paintings of
women (and, I learned later, by women), and plants gathered near the
long windows along the north side. It seemed as much a place for conversation as for writing. As I stood just inside the door, I could see people writing and talking about the writing they had done. What struck
me almost immediately was that I could not really tell the teachers from
the students. Nearly directly in front of me, three people were writing
at one of the round tables. All were apparently so involved with the
words they were putting on paper that no one looked up as the door
bounced shut behind me. Further into the room and to the right, four
people sat around another table. Two were talking. Rather, one was
talking and the other was listening. A third was writing and occasionally looking up and listening to the other two. The fourth person was
writing. At a table still further to the right and deeper into the room, no
one was writing. They all had slightly tattered sheets of paper full of
words in front of them. Often, their eyes and their fingers would point
to particular parts. Sometimes their talk would stop long enough for
one of them to read aloud something she had written, and then the talk

would begin again. The woman at the second table, the one who had been listening, looked over to me and smiled. She allowed the person talking to finish, said something brief in response, and stood up to walk over to meet me. She asked if she could help me. I told her that I wanted to teach in the Writing Lab and asked if she could introduce me to Lou Kelly, the Lab's director. She pointed to a large, steel-gray metal desk to the left and told me that the woman "hassling" (one of Lou's favorite words) someone for not writing more was her. An enduring and endearing relationship with Lou Kelly and the Writing Lab community began that day.

I wanted to participate in such a community—that was why I had entered graduate school. I entered the Writing Lab because, as a graduate student in my seminars, I had not yet found such a community. Those ways of writing and talking about writing were not the ones I wanted to be part of or participate in. I hoped instead that the Writing Lab would become the community I needed. I also hoped that the ways of writing and talking about writing in that Lab community would be both diverse and tolerant, embracing beginning writers and experienced writers, writers who were convinced (as I had been) that they were not, could not become writers, and writers for whom writing seemed their way of being in and a part of the world. I was rarely disappointed.

As with all communities, there were many "rules" for how one must act and interact in order to become a member. The first and foremost rule of the Writing Lab was to write and to write and to write. All were invited to fulfill what Lou believed were the original purposes of language, "the sharing of experience with others and responding to the experience others share with us." And this rule applied equally to the students and the teachers and the director. Lou was forever writing and sharing her writing with teachers and students in the Lab. She expected, demanded, the same of everyone else. The second rule and almost as important was to talk about writing. I wish that I could describe all those ways of talking about writing. I wish that I could point to the kinds of talk that helped both students and teachers to feel themselves part of something, but I cannot. There were, however, patterns in our talk. As students and teachers began to fill pages with writing and writing in response, our talk most often took the form of questions. Those questions were not at all unusual. They were very human, natural in the sense of being genuinely interested in someone else and wanting to know more and to understand better. They involved simply asking for more information: "Can you tell me more about the particular experience that has had such a dramatic effect on you?" or "Can you help me see what happened?" They involved asking writers to synthesize that information into a story, to articulate the relationships which determine the ordering of their ideas: "What have you learned through writing about your experience?" or "Has what you have learned changed your perception of that experience, of yourself and the others involved in that experience?" And those questions involved asking writers to speculate on the meaning(s) these shared experiences have for others: "What would you have others learn as they read of your experience?" Clearly, these questions are not unique. Still, each question (and the above examples represent neither the range nor the depth) served to confirm and affirm that the appropriate frame for understanding writing was the sharing of experience with others and responding to the experiences others share with us. Students writing led to teachers responding led to students writing more. In addition, students writing also led to other students responding, and teachers writing led to students responding. We all were writing, writing and talking in response, and always, always writing more. Through the acting and interacting that is writing and that surrounds writing with talk, we became a community of writers.

One example in particular of how our community of writers acted and interacted still remains quite vivid to me. It was not unusual for certain events or even local crises to become a temporary and very often intense focus of our writing and talking and writing more. Once, near the end of the semester, one of the black male student athletes on campus, a recent Writing Lab student, was accused of assaulting and raping a woman in her dorm. Many of the students knew the young man. All the teachers knew him. In the days immediately following the first newspaper reports, several students asked to write about this situation and shared their writing with their teachers and the other students. Many of the teachers also wrote and shared that writing with the students. The reactions to what was written and shared ranged from anger and outrage, to disbelief, to the felt need to defend and protect both the young woman and the young man. There were also students and teachers who wrote about their own experiences with rape. Some wrote about women they knew who had been raped. In fact, one of the women in the Writing Lab had been raped and wrote about it.

Eddie, another young black man, student athlete, and sometimes friend of the accused, wrote of the "groupies," young women that surround and flirt with male athletes. He wrote of the status these women gathered from being seen with the designated campus celebrities that athletes have now become. And he told stories of his experiences being "hussled." According to Eddie, it was not unusual for athletes the night after a game generally to be invited to a women's dorm or apartment: "They think you are a big deal," he wrote, "and who am I to tell them different." Angie, a young black woman, wrote of her disgust for athletes: "They think they're such big shits," she wrote. "All they think about is their own egos. Sure, it's kind of fun sometimes to get to know somebody who has been on TV or seems so popular, but they never get it through their hard heads that just because they're a jock doesn't mean that I want to sleep with 'em." Jane, on the other hand, was white and from a small rural community. She had never met an athlete and really wasn't interested in sports at all. She was interested in what had happened to the young woman and what could happen to her. She was frightened: "How can something like this happen in a dorm room," she asked in her writing. "Isn't there supposed to be some kind of security? Where were the other people on the dorm floor? Why didn't somebody come to help or call the police or something?" Ellie was a woman returning to school, a white "nontraditional student." She too was concerned for the young woman who had been raped. "I know something about how she might feel," she wrote. "Several years ago, I was raped, and I'm just now beginning to realize how what happened changed my life." Of course, there were others writing other reactions. Yet, these four students, along with another teacher and me, began to share our writing with one another. As a white male, I wrote that I had never known anyone or been aware that anyone I knew had been raped. I wrote that the only experience that I could use to help me understand what the violence of rape might be like was my own past involvement in a psychologically abusive relationship. I wrote, "I felt hated, or worse . . . made into an object of hate." Jennifer, the other teacher and a white woman, wrote of her growing understanding of rape through a book she had read by Susan Brownmiller, entitled *Against Our Will* (1975). She wrote of her anger and frustration: "I want to do something that will stop such a thing from ever happening again," she wrote, "but I don't know how."

All of us had stories to tell. Our first questions to each other asked for those stories. Eddie wrote of his experiences with the groupies, Angie with the jocks. I wrote of my past relationship, and Jennifer of her growing understanding of what rape really is and what she felt, knowing that this should reveal to us something about ourselves and our society. Jane wrote about how rape had always seemed to be something that happened somewhere else, to somebody else. She wondered now if that were really true. Ellie wrote of her experience. The questions continued. Jane asked Eddie if he thought the women he called groupies were really "asking for it." Eddie asked Angie if she thought that all athletes were "self-centered egomaniacs." Angie asked me how I understood what had happened to me as being "something really violent." Jennifer asked Ellie "to tell her of the ways your rape experience has changed your life." And Ellie asked for the titles of other books or articles Jennifer had read that had helped her better understand rape. The questions continued and so did our writing. Together, then, we began to ask questions about women's and men's roles in society and how those roles manifest themselves in labels like "groupies" or "jocks." We began to ask questions about race: "Why is it that when a black man rapes a white woman, it's headline news? Aren't white men raping white women or black women? Aren't black men raping black women? Why aren't these incidents headline news?" And we began to ask questions about violence: "What is violence? What is a violent act? Why do so many people disagree about what violence is?" And we continued to write.

For some of us, through our writing and talking and writing more, rape, specifically, and violence against women, generally, became a real concern to us for the first time, something immediate, real, and serious. For others, those for whom rape was already manifest, writing provided an opportunity to make public an experience and a response to that experience. Of course, not everyone agreed with what one another had to say. Neither did we—either in our small community of writers or in the larger community of writers that included everyone in the Lab—arrive at any sort of consensus about how we thought the society we all lived in should deal with this problem. Some in the Lab chose not to write about rape at all. Yet, through *Voices*, published excerpts of Lab students and teachers writing, everyone became involved, at least as readers. Our writing experience became a way of sharing experience with others and of responding to our writing. Because those ways of talking, our questions, suggested that we cared about what we were saying to one another, cared about what each of us was thinking, writing became a natural and necessary activity in our community. We became writers because we wanted and needed to write to each other. We wrote because we came to understand ourselves and each other as writers.

In every writing class I have been involved with since then, I have tried to foster a development of the understanding of one's self as a writer acting and interacting within a community of writers. For me, the keys to that development can be drawn from the preceding stories, which suggest something of my own development. We write only when we begin to understand ourselves and each other as participants in the world and writing and reading the writing of others as ways of participating. We become a community of writers only when we want and need to write to one another and read one another's writing, when the talk that surrounds that writing and reading genuinely engages ourselves and others and demands authentic response.

Ruth's Story: Connecting Groups In and Out of School— Locations for Learning

Before I moved to Florida, I thought only midwesterners had the habit of doggedly pursuing the possible geographic or social connections they might have with others, especially new acquaintances. Where I was born, raised, educated, or who I know, am related to, or married to often seemed more important to some people than the occasion that brought us together. But even here in the South, I've heard these conversations: "Oh, you went to school in Kentucky? Then you must know so-and-so" or "I was in your hometown once, twenty years ago—Say, you don't live near the airport, do you?" Despite the absurdity of some of these attempts, the pleasure of finding that we have a common acquaintance or know the same restaurant in a city far away immediately makes us more interested in continuing the relationship. These initial connections locate other people in our world: when we know *where* or *to whom* they belong, they become more significant, more memorable, more real in some sense to us as people.

My students try out locating conversations when they first meet in small groups, sometimes unsuccessfully. Students don't always have effective ways to deal with the artificial, forced membership and imposed tasks of small-group writing workshops, except to bring what they know of group processes from the outside. The locating conversations that work to make friends may or may not work in a group that is forced to work together and share texts. In many ways, what I see at work in effective small groups is a community "culture" which celebrates common goals while encouraging individuality. This kind of community culture is a distinctly different kind of community than the competitive, evaluative community I participated in during school hours. The difference is due in part to the place where the group forms, the locus and methods of its operation, as the history of small groups demonstrates (see Gere 1987, part I). Informal, spontaneous groups with volunteer membership are generally located in the world outside the classroom. However, for our students, the two locations for two kinds of small groups overlap in subtle and complex ways.

This sense of the location of a group becomes clear to me and to my students when we contrast how we function in the informal groups composed of our families and friends with how we function in the formal groups in school, both of which (especially for students whose social life is closely bound to school activities) can be composed of the same people. Much of what I find that "works" with small groups in my writing classes comes from initiating and formalizing the connections students have with each other as people, not just as fellow students. Telling my own story about connections with other people allows students to see how their own pasts have affected their attitudes and expectations toward group work in the writing class.

When my family gathers over the holidays at my parents' home in Oklahoma, we spend most of our time in the kitchen. We have often joked that we gravitate toward the kitchen because that's where the food is, but I believe the kitchen is the best place for talk because it groups us in circles, either around the cooking area or around the table. When I was growing up, meals eaten in the kitchen were the occasion for catching up on the days' plans or problems, complaining, telling stories, discussing issues. The tradition of the kitchen as the location for the work of my immediate family, especially as the "office" for the women of the family, comes from a longer tradition of my grandparents' family in rural western Oklahoma, in a time and place where the extended family had to work together in relative harmony in order to survive.

"People are joined to the land by work," writes Wendell Berry (1988, 50), and this kind of identity of location and action I observed when I visited my grandparents' farm during the wheat harvest in late May. My grandmother's home was always filled with people either working together or preparing to work together. Even children could be helpful during harvest, following my grandmother as she worked, gathering eggs and watering the vegetable garden. My sister and I, while washing a seemingly endless stream of dishes from the twenty people working the harvest, listened to the adults planning the day's work, negotiating varied skills and farm machinery, and arguing politics. Regular, hearty meals were important during harvest, not just for the food, but for the time to sit together and plan the next field to move equipment to, discuss the weather, speculate about the crop and the latest local gossip. Experiences of single individuals made good stories to tell around the dinner table, but the identity of the community came through group efforts to work the land. Members of the family or community who lived apart from the rest of the group or wanted to be alone for a short time or a lifetime were, in my family's opinion, considered lazy or just plain strange. Even reading silently, in the evening after chores were done, was more enjoyable when others were around to comment on what you were discovering in the text.

My own position within this extended family group has changed over the years, as does most membership in informal groups. As a child, my role in this group was that of observer and listener. When I was older, my grandmother reminded me that a woman's world was *"Küchen, Kinder, und Kirche"*—kitchen, children, and church. But my grandmother also knew that living on a farm in a solidly German-Lutheran community meant a woman's world was as physical and political as a man's world, and farm work never discriminated by sex. The roles in the small group that ran the farm were flexible, and the goal was clear but unarticulated. When my own educational and vocational goals would not allow me to stay in the area or understand the decisions being made, I had little to contribute to the farm and grew more distant from the farm community. Education was a benefit in the eyes of my grandparents, and they were always proud of my accomplishments, but they valued the kind of practical skill and knowledge which school doesn't teach. As I chose to move away or "dislocate" myself from one small group, I joined others, creating another family group.

Besides considering our families, my students and I have explored other influences on their sense of appropriate and inappropriate group processes. Sometimes students are less self-conscious telling each other about groups other than their immediate families, such as the "clique" groups that form in some high schools. For instance, because my father was a minister, the church was another site or location where I saw specialized groups working together in different ways. In the Lutheran churches to which my family belonged, all matters were handled formally by committees, but most decisions were actually made by informal groups such as the quilters who met every week in the church basement or the men standing together around the coffeepot after services. The quilters at one of our parishes spent every Thursday together, quilting for six to eight hours, and talking about everything that happened in the community, keeping track of the members, evaluating and explaining behavior, going over all the possible solutions to a problem, and finding the acceptable norms in everything. They talked at a level of detail we might call trivial—"Is Etta coming home from the hospital in the morning or the afternoon?" "Do you mix the eggs or cream the butter first?" "Will the church's linen tablecloth last through two more weddings this fall?"—but the talk kept the church running. Most decisions in the church were made this way, and the formal annual meetings of the congregation were a reaffirmation of those decisions. Thinking about these church groups led me to ask students: "Where and when did you learn how the system worked in a group? Were there proper and improper ways to make decisions in this group? Where did the real work get done?"

These kinds of stories of families and friends are familiar to only a few of my students, who also come from broken and blended families, urban and inner-city regions, well-educated and wealthy backgrounds, gangs and foster homes. Even students who consider themselves "loners" come to see their dislike of groups or ostracism from groups as powerful experiences. Minority students have particularly potent experiences of belonging and not belonging to groups.

However, many of my students' experiences in school have shaped their personalities as learners and thinkers just as strongly. Many students find their academic experiences in formal, task-oriented small groups touch most profoundly their attitudes toward writing and sharing work in a small group. My own school experiences parallel those of my students' fairly closely, and recounting them reminds me of how much of my frustration with small-group work originated in the dissonance and overlap between academic, structured groups and informal, unstructured groups. Even with all my experience in groups and in watching groups work in my family, the groups in school settings were difficult for me. Schoolwork and writing were about filling out work sheets and taking tests—two things I nearly always did alone (and was told to do alone)—so when I was involved in a group learning or group writing project, I was confused, and I thought mostly about the injustice of evaluating group learning. Performance and evaluation were the goals of school activities, I perceived. Group work in grade school and high school, I thought, led to nothing other than a watered-down version of what I could do better by myself, or it brought every member down to the lowest common denominator ("the laziest") in the group. Group work was never perceived by teachers or students as serious learning.

At Dana College, the small liberal arts college I attended, many academic courses involved small-group work for discussion or collaborative projects. Since the school was small, nearly all the students knew each other. I was regularly assigned to collaborative small groups with friends and acquaintances. In one instance, I was a small-group leader (not a volunteer) in a core humanities course. I didn't mind leading the group, but to be a part of the group and share ideas on an equal basis, and then to turn around and make decisions about grades and progress, seemed impossible to me. The role of discussion leader was a social one, where I called upon my personal knowledge of my classmates and relied on character traits and ways of thinking, while the role of evaluator the group meant being distant and objective, purposely forgetting any personal connections I had with the group.

The purpose of these college groups was hazy to me at best, and I felt I was receiving another mixed message, as well: guiding and organizing a small group and being a learning, contributing member of that group could not be combined roles in my experience. In school, the de facto leader of any group, whether present or not, was a teacher in a superior position who knew all the "right" answers the group members were to discover through discussion. These groups had nothing to do with the group work I saw at home around my family's kitchen table or the groups I saw on my grandparents' farm in Oklahoma. We didn't plan our time, we didn't meet over food and drink, and we didn't feel free to choose our roles.

On the other hand, I was certain that the small groups could be as interesting and productive as the group discussion my friends and I had in our dorm rooms and in the snack bar about the ideas we didn't quite understand, the assignments we hated, and what we thought we were going to do with our new knowledge. After all, the same people were walking from the snack bar to the classroom—why did the conversation become so much more labored and difficult in the classroom?

In graduate school, every group to which I was assigned in graduate seminars used the tactic of dividing the work into parts so that each member of the group could work on her own and be responsible for only her parts. Dividing responsibility made evaluation more or less "fair," but the method often backfired when we inadvertently prepared similar materials or when one member was absent for the dividing ceremonies. Essentially, we refused to work as a small group. In graduate school, though, I also discovered myself as a teacher, experimenting with all kinds of small groups, watching students work together in different ways, and finding out by trial and error what did and didn't work: students can't launch without preamble into effective discussion about any topic; students can talk intently about things they know something about; groups which work well one day may not work well every other day.

Gradually, I learned that I myself was not a very good group member. Although my family and my community taught me how to accomplish tasks in groups, they didn't teach me how to interpret the words or interrupt the speech of someone different from me, someone from outside my community or family. And yet, though so many of my own formal group experiences were negative, I recognized that I learned more and learned differently in informal small groups. The group learning which was exciting and provocative for me took place at the bar following graduate seminars, over lunch with fellow students, and in hallways or private conferences with my students. Being responsible for what I did and didn't know, finding ways to express what was important to me, hearing other students' perspectives and connections with new knowledge, arguing and debating issues were all potentially powerful interactions in informal small groups and made my discomfort with formal groups more and more puzzling. The question kept coming back to me: there had to be ways to reproduce the context of familiar, informal small groups, which my students had all experienced, in the classroom.

When I claimed my personal life as a valuable learning experience, I worked harder to find the relationship between formal and informal groups. When I started graduate school the second time around, I read more about small groups, such as Elbow's *Writing without Teachers* (1973). In a graduate seminar in composition, I found myself in a small group of graduate students, this time without the option of dividing the work and working alone. This writing workshop group, modeled after the workshop in the National Writing Project, consisted of a Benedictine monk, an older Chinese student who had left his family behind in China, another fellow graduate teaching assistant, and me. Wenxiong brought narratives about surviving the oppressive Cultural Revolution in China, Father Denis brought long intensely personal poems about his mother, Tom brought pieces of fiction about adolescent males, and I brought book reviews: none of us was exactly sure what we as a group were "supposed" to do. We were wary of each other and uncertain about showing anyone our "creative" writing, but by halfway through the semester, we finally got to know each other well enough to respond as readers. There was no sudden epiphany, but one day the workshop just felt comfortable to all of us. We tended to talk about ourselves more than about our writing because we honestly couldn't understand each other's writing without help. This small group taught me that small groups have to talk about themselves enough to understand why they write and what they are trying to accomplish in their writing. They have to know each other's attitudes and goals, initiating and interrupting habits, tolerance levels and peacekeeping abilities. In other words, small-group members must know each other's situation in the context of the writing. Just as a teacher doesn't know what to do with a student text which doesn't follow the assignment and shows no connection to the student's experiences, small-group members don't know what to do with each other's writing if they don't know what the text, either literally or emotionally, means to the writer. Lucy Mc-

Cormick Calkins (1991) describes what a small group needs as "that spirit, that intimacy, [which] comes from sharing bits of life" (20).

Shortly after working with Wenxiong, Denis, and Tom, I began participating in a research project on small groups for which I read reams of transcripts of recorded small groups as they worked in college composition courses. In the transcripts, I saw how students work out ways to deal with their very different backgrounds as writers and students, even when they don't seem to be doing anything but talking about the latest campus scandal. They were doing their best to bring their knowledge of small groups' behavior to the artificial nature of assigned small groups, the same struggle I'd had all along.

Informal and formal small groups are vastly different locations for learning. All teachers and students have family and friendship experiences of some sort, and they have ideas about how people should get along. Sometimes I want my students to consider their small group as a kind of family: a group of people they didn't choose to be associated with and with whom they may radically disagree, but whom they respect as people and writers, and whom they treat as such. Some of the guidelines and rules I set up for small groups in my classroom derive quite directly from my experiences in groups that were comfortable and focused. However, my primary reason for recalling and reclaiming my past experiences in small groups is to encourage and model the same actions in my students. Now, I see my students and I struggling together to transform informal and natural knowledge and experience into useable formal and artificial behavior in the classroom. The point is not that anyone has a special background that helps students imitate a kind of small-group culture, but that "we are all at once both insiders and outsiders," as Joseph Harris (1989) argues. "The task facing our students . . . is not to leave one community in order to enter another, but to *reposition* themselves" (19; his italics), or to re-locate themselves in the various communities they encounter, including structured, school-sponsored groups. The question isn't "So where do I think my students are or should be?" asked of me as teacher, but rather "Where are you?" posed directly to the students.

Conclusion: Writing Groups and Life Experience

As these stories make clear, the three of us—from very different pasts—have come to use writing groups as a part of our pedagogy. Ruth's past was dominated by the informal groups of the small town, the family farm, and the Lutheran church, yet her school experience was predominately individual and evaluative, with groups functioning informally outside the classroom (if they functioned at all). For her to find ways of bringing small groups into her writing classroom has meant finding ways of valuing those formative nonacademic elements of her past and seeing how their values and assumptions can contribute to the lifelong task of learning. Rick's past, by contrast, is marked by the transformative experiences of working with one extraordinary professor and then working in Iowa's Writing Lab—experiences which changed writing from something he was endlessly evaluated as "not being good at," to a way of participating in an active, diverse community. For him to bring small groups into his classrooms has meant trying to capture those elements of his experience that made school a transformative instead of restrictive place, those elements that made writing and reading shared, participatory experiences instead of solitary, evaluative ones. Unlike Ruth or Rick, Robert experienced writing groups from an early age as a primary way of forming friendships, connecting with people, and producing work his community cared about; writing groups were, for him, a site half-in and half-out of school, where his most important social and vocational development occurred. For Robert to bring small groups into his writing classes has meant his trying to share that social and vocational development with students, to invite them to experience writing as a means of connecting with people and producing work they and their communities value.

As we'll go on to describe in subsequent chapters, the particular pedagogies we've developed from our experiences with groups are somewhat different, emphasizing the elements of writing groups that most connect with our personal pasts. We believe that, as teachers, we cannot do otherwise—our lives and our teaching are not separate realms, but ones which intersect and support each other in many ways. In the stunning images of Mary Catherine Bateson (1989) and Bettina Aptheker (1989), our academic lives are interwoven with our lives outside of school just as the strands of a web or the threads of a tapestry are interwoven, and our best teaching emerges from a sympathetic acceptance of the interdependence of these strands. To write this book together, remaining aware of our three unique perspectives (as well as the many principles we share), we've needed to discuss and understand the individual pasts that have influenced our use of small groups in writing classrooms. Any teacher's use of small groups depends similarly on a sympathetic understanding of the ways such groups have influenced his or her own development in and out of school. Our profession's general call for small-group pedagogy, we believe, requires such sympathetic understanding of our own past lives.

II Pedagogy

Introduction

One of the typical encounters we have with other teachers about small groups goes like this: We are invited to speak about small groups. We prepare a talk which explains our philosophies about small groups—their importance to learning and especially learning to write, the connections and misconnections between small groups and conventional wisdom about writing development and writing instruction. Then we present our ideas in front of an alert, interested audience. At the close of our talk, we ask for questions. Inevitably, the first questions are not about why one might adapt or invent a pedagogy which includes small groups but rather about what we call the "nuts and bolts": "How often should I rearrange the students into different groups?" or "What do you do with a student who is never prepared for group work?" or "What do I say to a student who thinks other students' responses to her writing are like the blind leading the blind?" These "How do I . . . " questions are the ones most immediately problematic for all of us, and they are as perplexing and challenging as the "Why should I . . . " questions.

The chapters in this section of the book are intended to answer those "nuts and bolts" questions in the context of our ideas about why one bothers with small groups in the first place. We have found that the more mechanical matters usually fall into place once we have a fairly firm idea of how our philosophy of small groups (how they can and do work) meshes with our philosophy of writing pedagogy. Each of the next three chapters describes an individual teacher's ways of handling small groups, emphasizing the way that our respective pedagogies developed out of a particular idea of the purposes for groups in writing instruction. In chapter 4, Ruth Mirtz shows how her use of small groups has developed over time based on the mental model of small-group interaction she held in her head as teacher. In chapter 5, Robert Brooke describes the ways small groups support the general invitation to a writer's life that he extends to his students. In chapter 6, Rick Evans traces the way he uses small groups to help would-be writing teachers claim their own uses of writing and the transformative power of the English classroom. Chapter 7 presents, in question-and-answer format, many of our joint answers to the questions we most often hear about small-group work. Chapter 8 discusses the reality of making changes toward small-group pedagogy in situations that discourage change and innovation.

We offer these descriptions as suggestions and as possible inspiration for innovation, not as required scripts for successful small groups. We are constantly adapting our classes and our small-group pedagogy to the environment and the situations in which we find ourselves and our students, and we expect our readers will do the same.

4 Model Groups and Un-Model Writers: Introducing First- and Second-Year College Students to a Writer's Life

Ruth Mirtz
Florida State University

One of the ways in which I have decided to handle small groups over my twelve years of teaching is through *models*. I have operated with certain idealized forms of how I thought small groups ought to work and how I should relate to those small groups. Each model I have used, consciously or not, has a guiding purpose and is a mode of instruction, requires different classroom management skills, comes with a certain set of problems, and issues certain invitations to a writer's life.

If I tried to imagine today what an ideal small group would look like and how this ideal small group would act, I would imagine something like this:

> The first day of my first-year composition class, I enter my classroom five minutes early and find the students have moved the chairs into a circle. They are introducing themselves to each other, discovering what parts of the country and state they are from and what other classes they are taking this semester, commiserating that they couldn't get into the classes they really wanted. When I describe the workshop format of the class, they nod their heads and look at each other knowingly (they will have all experienced this form of class work in high school, of course). The second day of class, I go to the classroom five minutes early again, and the students are already in small groups of four or five, looking at copies of each others' writing assignment for the day. One group has realized that they are imperfectly balanced with men and women and that two of the four women are close acquaintances from their high school. They are negotiating a change of members with the group next to them. Another group, meeting close to the door to the hallway, catches me as I come in and asks how much time they have to respond to the writing assignment because one member has volunteered to keep time. I pull up a chair into a group with only four members and listen to their discussion of what might be helpful ways of responding to this particular writing assignment.

Wouldn't it be wonderful?

This story may seem like a complete and utter fantasy, but some semesters this does actually happen in my classes by midsemester, although never during the first two class sessions. What this story describes is the model of small groups I am operating with: small groups are self-motivated, able to discuss and determine their own operating procedures, have a repertoire of responding techniques and conflict-management methods and can invent new ones, know the value of other writers' responses and understand the influence of the presence and response of other writers on their writing. The fantasy is the part about how my students come to my class already knowing all these things; the reality is that I must provide the kinds of experience and guidance that allow them to develop or discover these things on their own. Another reality is that not all students will learn these things no matter what I do in the classroom, because a student's prior experiences with writing and small-group work are often stronger than the ones I arrange or happen upon by accident in the course of the semester.

Before I describe how I use this model of small groups, I want to describe some of the other models I have used and how they worked, a narrative of missteps and misunderstandings. You may recognize some elements of your own model in some of these descriptions. Because I tend to be a visual learner and because at heart I am an idealist, developing a model for my teaching helps me to articulate my pedagogy and determine better or best methods as well as to invent new methods to experiment with. As Ann Berthoff (1981) has suggested, models are meaning-making symbols (7); models inform our teaching and are formed by our teaching experiences. The more models we as teachers are familiar with, the more we can understand the model our students are using, because students operate with models, too, formed from their past experiences. In a small group, they will act upon and experiment with models similar to the ones I describe below. An important part of a student's development as a writer is her negotiation of her role within a model of small-group behavior.

Thinking with Models (Minding Models)

My own story of change starts with some typical, uncomfortable small-group experiences as a student. My family moved frequently when I was in grade school, and I was regularly assigned to do projects with other students, projects which often seemed much harder because of the need to collaborate with students I didn't know very well. Like many children, I was shy, but I wanted to do well in school and please my teachers. Since I was usually an outstanding student academically and behaviorally, I received a certain amount of unwelcome attention from my classmates. No one likes the "teacher's pet," and that was the only role that seemed, to me, available for students who were bright, well-behaved, and terribly shy. I must have seen much of my schoolwork as a competition for the teacher's attention. Other students could act out to get the teacher's attention; I could only do better and better on exams and papers. But in group projects, I didn't know how to act. I couldn't get the individual attention in the ways to which I was accustomed, and I wasn't any good at working with other children. In general, I avoided group work whenever I could. My model of small groups was "forced interaction with other students."

During high school and college, general adolescent turmoil turned a dislike for academic group work into an unfocused dread. I felt that because of my academic reputation, I was always unfairly called upon by teachers and fellow students to lead the group work. Despite the positive small-group experiences I described in chapter 3, I've probably overcompensated in my teaching by stressing the goal of small groups in my own teaching. I am also acutely aware of the issue of fairness in small groups—one reason why I have never considered giving "group grades," even though I have heard colleagues describe their successes with it.

I've described these childhood and adolescent "models" of small groups because they had a significant impact on my ideas of what is just and because they color my particular sympathies for students who have had similar experiences with small groups. The influence of my formal teacher training (sporadic and superficial) is not nearly as great. In college education courses, I learned just enough about John Dewey and Maria Montessori to understand the importance of direct application of new knowledge—that in order to truly learn anything it must be internalized as a part of the learner's real world.

When I began teaching a course in humanities at the University of Nebraska at Omaha (an interdisciplinary "heritage of western civilization" course), small groups were a shortcut, a way to individualize instruction and make historical and remote issues more immediate by asking students to discuss these issues among themselves and to share their understanding and experiences. More practically, small-group discussion forced students to do their homework and to participate more actively in the class.

The humanities course was organized into a large lecture section and many smaller sections of discussion groups. Each smaller section had thirty to thirty-five students, though, so discussion had to take place in even smaller groups to ensure full participation. The goal of the course was to produce "cultured," liberally educated citizens who could critique the white, male, western influences on their lives, who knew a broad range of general philosophies and critical theories, who had a sense of the sweep of world history, and who maybe even enjoyed going to an art exhibit or a music concert. The small discussion groups were essential for reaching those goals and ensuring that the students didn't just soak in all the information we threw at them without thinking and writing about it. Typical discussion instructions might be to describe and discuss Pico della Mirandola's Renaissance interpretation of "man" as the measure of all things, whether or not the students agreed with Mirandola, and what other "measures" might exist for modern culture.

The model I operated with was one that assumed students came to college-level work with well-developed, small-group communication skills which instantly translated into small-group discussion skills. This model said that members of small groups openly share opinions and knowledge, confident that they will not be criticized or denigrated for mistakes or differences of opinion and background. The goal of small groups in this model is increased understanding and a wider perspective on issues. My role was to push the conversation in the groups further into complex issues and to help keep the conversation going. The guidelines I offered were usually questions the group should try to answer about a certain subject, always including questions which applied the subject matter to the students' own experiences and values.

Sometimes these discussion groups worked well. However, my students were not confident of their knowledge and did not have well-developed opinions on the topics the course required them to discuss. When one member of the group was unprepared on the subject, that member usually remained silent. When most or all of the group were unprepared, they had to cover their lack of discussion, or I had to give them a revised assignment. It was also apparent that students who were well-prepared but were quiet or less easily sociable with strangers had a difficult time in these small groups. The model placed the blame for poor group discussion on student preparation of the immediate material. Yet, in individual discussions with students where I could draw out a student's knowledge, they did indeed have ideas about their lives and the cultures surrounding them.

When I started teaching composition at the University of Nebraska–Lincoln, the goal of small groups in my classroom changed from discussion to response to texts, and I ran up against new problems. In a discussion group, the typical first topic was shared complaints about the difficulty of the text, how boring the previous lecture had been, how little of the assignment they'd actually read. But when the students responded to each other's writing, I knew no precedent for helping small groups introduce shared attitudes and experiences. Instead, I thought a peer-response group would launch immediately into polite, diplomatic constructive criticism and after a few weeks of guidance and practice, would give analytic criticism to each other which would help students revise and improve their papers. What really happened was that my small groups consistently worked off-task (refusing to do what I asked them and discussing everything but their papers) or ripped each other's papers apart (causing hard feelings and outright rebellion).

The model I was using placed students as substitute teachers who did some work for the teacher and supposedly had the same level of knowledge about the topics and organization as the teachers. Students, again theoretically, came to the class as well-formed writers with completely developed skills in working with strangers and were relatively static in development over the course of the semester. If a group was not very successful at responding, then they were not motivated or had personality conflicts. My role, therefore, was to motivate students (usually through punitive grading) and to arrange personalities into nonconflictive groups.

In practice, a typical small-group session would begin with students looking at each other and wondering what to do first. Then, one brave student would point out a grammatical error and the whole group would argue about how to correct the error. Or another student would say something like, "I think you should write more about this part," and the writer would reply that then the paper would be too long or that she didn't have any more to say about that part. Then, the next student, feeling the writer was getting picked on, would say, "I liked your paper a lot. You should leave it just the way it is." And then the group would move on to the next student's paper.

In addition to my goals for the small-group-as-critical-team, I also expected the groups to act as helpful co-writers. I told them that small groups gave them a chance to "cheat legally," by getting help on their papers from their group members. The students should relate similar experiences, ask questions, develop arguments, and give advice. Most groups could do this, but they tended to wander into long discussions about things not directly related to their papers. The collaborative work felt like a gab session to most students, so it turned into one. Plus, my directions for giving "advice" and for giving "help" conflicted. Students weren't sure whether they were supposed to describe what they thought was good or bad about a paper or to tell the writer what to do. After a few weeks of asking the students what their conversations had to do with their papers, they would volunteer explanations: "We're working, we really are." My role turned into a taskmaster almost immediately.

The model of the small-group-as-collaborative-team assumes that writers easily share knowledge as co-writers, are experienced with making decisions by group consensus while respecting the minority's decisions, and again are relatively static in their development: they come to my course well formed in these areas and only need my assignments and evaluation process to motivate them to use these well-formed skills. As in the model of the small-group-as-critical-team, if a group doesn't get along and succeed in helping to improve each other's writing, it's because of personality conflicts or lack of motivation.

At this point, I reached an impasse. If I set rigid rules for how and when to respond to texts, students would most likely take the least thoughtful and safest recourse and do only exactly what I required, like filling out a workbook response sheet, and I would end up doing most of the critical responding myself, thereby limiting the students to only my perspective on their texts. If I fell back on my earlier models, students still lost the added experience of multiple interpretations of their texts and focused solely on my authoritarian interpretation. The models I had used thus far made me too much the authority in each small group and ultimately felt like small-group work was simply a shuffle in classroom furniture instead of a true teaching method.

There were other options, too, though, such as adding a group grade as part of the individual grades as added incentive, or responding to texts as a large group or between students in pairs. But after reading Peter Elbow's *Writing without Teachers* (1973) and being in a peer-response group myself, I changed from using small groups as collaborators or as critics to using small groups for response. A peer-response group acts as a group of honest, critical, yet encouraging readers. Readers tell the student writer what they understood, what confused them, what they think the writer is saying or trying to say. Then the writer decides what to do about revising toward those responses. Peer responders try not to say what writers should do, but what writers could do. The model that results places the teacher as a fellow writer, who can model both writerly response and helpful small-group behavior. The audience for the writing assignment becomes the small group, rather than the non-existent "general reader" or the teacher herself.

This worked a great deal better in my classes, but it required a lot of modeling and direction (actually, rules about which responses are allowed and which aren't). The small-group-as-peer-readers confuses students who aren't accustomed to reading carefully and who are unsure about the difference between their emotional response to a piece and an emotional evaluation of a piece. This type of small group also limits the role of small-group members by eliminating evaluation and editing. For most of my students, it means learning new ways of talking about someone else's writing.

What made this model more successful was my own experience in a group of this type, which forcefully showed me how small groups can work—the group of Wenxiong, Denis, Tom, and me. In a graduate class, I was forced to pretend for half a semester that I was a writer, a writer who enjoyed and benefited from the response of other writers, who was a willing responder to others' writing. During the second half of the semester, I didn't have to pretend. I did feel like a writer, and I did enjoy the response. I felt that I could improve my writing in ways not possible without the group. The model became an experience I wanted to recreate for my students rather than being an instructional model which I had always hated as a student myself. My individual work remained in my control and in my hands but was in a willing dialogue with other writings and other writers.

At the same time that I was making this shift, I began a research project in which I closely studied transcripts from several small groups in composition classes as they met over the course of a semester. The transcripts revealed a number of things going on in small groups that I hadn't noticed before, such as struggles to agree on an interpretation of the task I had given them, struggles to present themselves as competent students and writers but also more than just students and writers, struggles to find a procedure which allowed each member to stay in control and meet his or her own needs while helping the others, and so on. These struggles were partly necessitated simply by being a small group by force rather than by choice and partly by being expected to respond not only to each other but also to each other's texts. Textual representations of their roles as students, writers, and authorities on their own experiences added a layer of negotiation particularly difficult for me to deal with on the level of rules and expectations. In a way, their texts gave them less space to retreat to; because they had to share their texts in one way or another, they couldn't choose not to be heard, and they were forced to voice themselves in a medium they were less experienced with than speaking, dressing, gesturing, etc.

The group we studied often seemed to be "off-task." For example, in the following dialogue, the group is discussing Jeff's draft about when he had to decide which college to attend and which college football team to play for:

> *Jeff:* Oh, I'm sorry, go ahead.
>
> *Renee:* Um, uh, I think that [garbled] and you have a really good topic, but there's certain parts you could elaborate on, you know—
>
> *Jeff:* [laughs]
>
> *Renee:* It's a good—you know—
>
> *Jeff:* I know. She told me that last week [laughs]
>
> *Renee:* I memorized it. I, you know, I just tell you that every week. No . . . for instance—
>
> *Jeff:* Uh, it is short. It is short.
>
> *Renee:* You know, like that part—
>
> *Chuck:* It doesn't matter how long it is.
>
> *Jeff:* Um-hmm.
>
> *Renee:* No—
>
> *Mike:* Let her, let her talk.
>
> *Jeff:* Go ahead.
>
> *Renee:* [laughs] The part about getting letters, I thought you could tell, like, who your first letter was from, and what, you know [pause] where is that part?
>
> [pause]
>
> *Mike:* Sounds like you're receiving the first letter from the Cornhuskers. You know. You forgot totally about the first couple of letters in between. Maybe you should name some of the bigger schools.

Renee offers generic encouragement, gets teased about it, gets interrupted several times, and suggests added details for the text. Chuck offers advice about the assignment. Mike tries to control the talking and the turn taking, and responds to his reading of the text and gives a suggestion for additional information. In the space of a few short moments, the group has worked through conflicts, renegotiated leadership, and responded to both writing and attitudes. However, the methods they used were humor and indirection, which often confused them and in the classroom appeared "off-task" to their instructor.

Reading these transcripts was an eye-opening extension of my knowledge about what students do in reaction to these artificial small groups. I realized that I had little idea what students did in small groups when I wasn't present, how they interpreted and misinterpreted instructions and comments. I realized I needed to listen more to small groups and interrupt less with my own, better advice and response to their texts. More and more, I asked open-ended questions ("So, how are you doing here?") which required students to report or give a version of their functioning and accomplishments in their own terms, rather than mine. More importantly, I defined a "successful" group differently. In the past, a successful group, for me, had been a group which did what I would do—responded to texts in the same teacherly ways, forming the same teacherly relationship between group members. Now, instead of seeing small groups as off-task or a failure, I saw small groups as a locus for writerly behavior. Students were uneducated or inexperienced in the ways to respond to texts as the focus of a small-group community rather than lazy or uninterested. Studying small groups through the transcripts and in my own classes made me realize the diverse and conflicting expectations and backgrounds of the students in my classes. My long-held feelings about what was "fair" about small groups surfaced, and I realized this model offered me a way to help students work together well in small groups without resorting to punitive evaluation measures, such as giving a "group grade" to ensure that each member has a stake in the success of the group.

My role changed from making all the students act and think alike to giving them ways to communicate and regulate their dissimilarities. That meant providing ways to hear each other's versions of what was happening in their group, why each one wrote what he or she did, and why each wanted or needed a particular kind of response and advice. In addition to needing a common ground of experiences, small groups which respond to texts must expect differences and disagreements. A teacher discovers individual and group needs and points them out (or helps the students to discover them) by making small groups a subject of discussion, asking questions, offering alternative strategies to manage disagreements, all in the context of responding to texts.

Changing to the model of the small-group-as-arena-of-role-experimentation involved a movement from viewing groups as static to viewing them as dynamic; from the group goal of becoming more the same to a group goal of negotiating differences; from the group purpose of improving each other's texts to the group purpose of experimenting with being a writer instead of only a student. Each group "invents" itself, each group find its own way to meet diverse and conflicting goals, and each individual modifies her personal goals to some extent to make the group work. This last model is also a change in the kind of model: all my previous models were models of *kinds* of students, rather than a kind of *development* in students.

One More Model and a Caveat

During my last year at the University of Nebraska–Lincoln, I taught in the Writing Center. Most of my students worked individually, but some students who had similar interests and needs worked together in what we named a "writer's circle." I was a member of the circle and wrote and responded along with the students. I set up the group initially along the lines of a peer-response group—each week, one or two members give copies of their work to the other members and ask for certain kinds of response. While we did respond to the poems, short stories, and passages of prose, we did more talking about writing than any other group I've ever been in or supervised as a teacher. We also planned several sessions where we wrote together instead of responding to texts. The writer's circle followed the model of a support group more than a response group.

Many of the small groups in my classes, especially groups which unanimously use a "family and friends" metaphor for their small group, are largely support groups. Every text and every experience is valued and encouraged and sympathized with. Each member is equal in value, and a leader's role is to make sure that the equality translates into equal time and equal support. They tend to talk more about their feelings toward their writing and the experiences they are describing in their writing—in fact, they often cannot move to the response guidelines until they have first talked about their emotional reactions to the writing or reading of texts.

I've only become aware of the importance of the support-group model for students in the last year or so, proving to myself yet again that there is more to learn about small-group behavior from students themselves. Models, however, have drawbacks. They tend to oversimplify many small-group processes. Small-group research in several fields tries to formulate models, without much far-reaching success, because of the tendency to oversimplify.[1] Such research also leads us to think that discovering the underlying model is the most important thing to know about a small group, when in fact the small group will be better off discovering for itself its own ways of functioning, whether the members choose to think in terms of models and metaphors or not. In actuality, models don't provide the dynamic, transformative information that experience does. I needed the support of models when I began teaching, but now, with more contact, observation, and thought, the sum of my experiences with students in small groups and as a member of small groups becomes the groundwork of my ideas and philosophy about small groups and teaching. The models assist me, more than direct me.

A Composition Class Based on Small-Group Work

The success of small groups in my first- and second-year composition classes seems to come from a blend of tight structure and nearly complete freedom, some close monitoring of what small groups are doing and some complete lack of monitoring. At some points during the semester (particularly the first few weeks) I give detailed, exact instructions about what small groups should and shouldn't do. At other times, I tell students that they should decide in their small groups how to deal with an assignment or how to work together on a project. Often, providing structure or monitoring makes certain options available to a small group to use if they feel they need them, with the option of ignoring or amending them when necessary.[2]

The First Day

The first day of class is often the most important in terms of setting the stage for small-group work. The first day is set aside for the usual read-through of the syllabus and the requirements, for introductions, and for first experiences in a new small group.

I arrange my composition courses into weekly workshops concurrent with weekly revisions of papers. One day a week is set side for small-group workshops centered around drafts. I assign periodic "final draft" due dates, usually three times during the semester, when a portfolio including journals, in-class writing, drafts, and at least one polished paper (the "final") are due. Students have certain freedoms: they are free to choose their own topics, revise one topic as often as they wish, and to choose a new topic when they feel ready. They have certain constraints: topics need to remain within the limits which we discuss as a class, such as avoiding excessive and gratuitous explicit sex and violence or one-sided denigrating topics; they need to keep me informed of their progress through drafts and toward final papers through conferences or letters; they need to consider the impact of their individual writing process on their ability to meet due dates and to work in a small group of other writers. Due dates and individual conferences allow me to exert considerable influence on their writing progress if necessary, and I respond regularly to their papers in addition to the responses they receive from the small-group workshops.

I make certain promises to the students on the first day of class: no one will be subjected to negative criticism of his or her writing; no one is forced to use the advice and response of the small group; the motivation and preparation of each small group member will be taken into account when I evaluate the success of the group (in other words, no hidden "group grades").

I give this kind of information on the first day of class so that students are informed of what will be required of them and to begin building their trust in my sense of evenhandedness and flexibility. What's more important on the first day of class is to begin the way we intend to continue: to act as writers in the presence of other writers. In other words, students need to both write and to have a successful small-group experience on the first day of class. I prefer to start strong by forming permanent small groups and giving a get-acquainted type of assignment for the small group, rather than a full-fledged workshop.

In the most typical scenario, I ask students to write briefly about themselves, warning them that they will be asked to hand in their writing. I might ask them to describe themselves in a certain way, to explain why they are in this class and what they think this class might be like. I count off the students into groups of three or four (never five, because of time constraints). The random counting removes responsibility for who ends up with whom from anyone or any circumstance; randomness also breaks up any pairs or groups of friends. Each group selects a "timekeeper" who makes sure everyone's writing receives equal time and a "leader" whose only assigned role is to make sure everyone has a chance to talk—usually by politely directing the talk away from a constant talker to a quiet member who may need some "airtime." I ask each group to introduce themselves, to read or report on what they wrote about themselves, discuss whatever similarities and differences they find in their backgrounds or ideas about this class, and to formally introduce one of their small group members to the rest of the class. This plan means that students write, listen to other writers, respond in small groups, and speak to the large group of the whole class, all on the first day of the course.

Workshops

Most of the difficult work of the small groups in my classes, that is, keeping the writer in control and making small-group behavior conscious, takes place during workshops. Each student brings copies of her draft for the other small-group members, reads her piece out loud, offers time for group members to reread and reflect before responding, and then asks for kinds of response within the guidelines I've given them.

The guidelines for response generally follow a development toward more and more detailed, readerly response, but they include certain absolute rules: no negative comments, only "I" statements ("I didn't understand this part" or "I'm confused here"). The guidelines begin with ways to make positive response: "What did/will you remember the most and why? What struck you the most forcefully and why? What did you like the best and why?" After two or three weeks, I offer other kinds of response: "What did you *get* from the text? What do you think the main point might/could be? What were you thinking during a particular part of the text?" Later in the semester, I offer even more detailed kinds of response: "If this were your paper, what would you do next?" As soon as possible, I suggest that students choose which kinds of response will help them the most, to talk first about how they feel and what they think about their text, to specifically ask for a kind of response from their small group, and to press their small group both to give the kind of response that will help them revise and refrain from less helpful kinds of response. (See figures 1–3 in chapter 5.)

Without guidelines and some mild enforcement of them, students will respond in the ways they've learned from other small-group experiences, usually by giving teacherly advice in the form of "you should" statements or by not responding at all. To help them prepare for workshops, I ask students to write down on their drafts three or four questions they want to ask their small group. After their workshop, they may write the same or other questions for me to respond to when I read their papers. I also model this procedure, trying out new response techniques by bringing my own short pieces of writing to class and using them as "practice" pieces.

Unless several students drop the course late in the semester or the class makeup changes drastically for some reason, I resist changing the small groups. My students stay in the same small groups all semester. When I ask them, the students themselves nearly always want to stay with the people they know, even when they don't get along very well. Students learn more about themselves, their writing and responding processes, and small-group communication, by sticking with a group, resolving conflicts and improving the small group, even if by small degrees.

Monitoring Small Groups

Because my students don't arrive in my class with fully developed skills in small-group work, I need to monitor all the small groups. Each small group, during the first two or three meetings, works out a way to proceed—they negotiate their roles in the group. They may or may not follow any advice or instruction I give them but still develop a functional way to operate. During workshop sessions, I "float" as a small-group member, not to "correct" their negotiations, but to be a part of them. I try to visit two or three groups during each workshop session. My coming and going seems disruptive at first, but the small groups adapt to it easily and sometimes specifically ask me to visit their small group first. I prefer to float so that I can stay a partial member of each group and be a part of the ongoing negotiations. As reading the research transcripts has taught me, I can't help students get along in their small groups if I don't understand the dynamics of the group. As a floating member of each small group, I am part of the negotiations, and I must also find a workable identity as a writer and as a teacher in that group. However, I have to stay in one group long enough to hear and observe their interaction and participate in that interaction. I have to remember to listen as well as talk. Bringing my own writing to each group makes my role as a fellow writer much easier. Generally, I spend a significant amount of time with one group as a fellow writer and responder, which allows me to model for each group a certain kind of small-group behavior. I stop briefly with the other groups and ask them, "How are things going?" This question is intended to illicit a report on what's happened so far in the group. Generally, the leader of the group will give his or her version and then the others will chime in with additional information or a different version.

Besides my direct presence as a monitoring device, I also periodically ask students to write to me about their small groups. (Most of the examples of students' responses in this chapter and chapter 2 were written first for monitoring purposes.) Small groups which consistently finish early can write quick reports after each workshop. By midsemester, at least, I ask all the students to respond in writing to questions like these: "Who is the leader in your group? What is your role in the group? How does your small group make decisions or resolve conflicts? What is your group good at and not so good at? What do you wish your small group did differently?" Some groups of students can share diplomatically worded versions of these responses with each other; other groups cannot.

Writing about one's small group is another way to openly present group behavior as a matter of concern to fellow writers, as a class and as a small group. I commonly present a new response technique, such as Elbow's "movie of the mind" (1981, 255), with questions such as "When would you want to ask for this kind of response from your small group? What if they say they don't know? What could you say if someone in your small group keeps pointing out your spelling errors after you've asked for movie-of-the-mind responses?"

Other Group Activities

One of my goals is to balance small-group work with individual conferences, individual private writing time, and large-group work. On the days when students aren't workshopping drafts of papers, I may introduce new invention and revision techniques, present a short text for discussion or analysis, ask students to prepare panel discussions or open-forum discussions, and take up topics of concern to a writer's life such as procrastination and writer's block. I often ask students to analyze their literacy, their reading and writing history, or their writing process; to set short-term and long-term goals; and to respond to what we do in class in order to give me a sense of what is and isn't working.

In nearly all these activities, I plan in-class writing to be shared in small groups. These kinds of writing require responding as fellow writers and students but not as critical readers, as they do during workshops. Meeting with other students in different groupings for sharing experiences and ideas (especially after midterm) helps students gain perspective on their group and meet others in the class.

How One Small Group Experienced Their Class

Even with a great deal of monitoring and modeling on my part, the small-group process tends to be spurred by past experiences and by what happens when I am not a member of the small group. It isn't unusual for a group to report that everything is going well and to be producing well-crafted papers when there are considerable unresolved conflicts in the group. Neither is it unusual for the members of a small group to give very different versions of what their small group is doing, as in the following example.

Karen, Marilyn, David, and Jeff were randomly assigned to a small group the first day of a second-year composition class. Karen was a sophomore transfer student from Norfolk College and wrote about her decision to come to the university, about how she and her father have battled their smoking habit, and a fictional story based on a daydream. Marilyn was a first-year student athlete from rural Nebraska who cracked one of her foot bones during the semester and lost four to six weeks of track practice and competition. She drew the cover for our class collection of papers. David was a senior ROTC student from Washington who told the class on the first day of school that he had more friends in the Persian Gulf than he had in the U.S. He seemed committed to the military life but wrote a paper about his experiences which revealed his mixed feelings about that lifestyle. During the semester, David learned that he narrowly made it into the navy program he was studying for. Jeff came to class the first week, then missed three weeks, then returned sporadically for two or three weeks, then disappeared altogether. He participated when he was present, but we learned almost nothing about him except that he wrote imaginative, interesting rough drafts. The other three were "good students"—good attendance, work handed in on time and complete, participation in large-group discussions. Marilyn and Karen received "B+'s," David a "B," Jeff an "F."

Each student here reports a different experience in the same small group. I would have agreed with Marilyn that they did too little direct responding about drafts. But I was always pleased with how they handled the mysterious Jeff. When he showed up, they were friendly and acted as if he had never been gone, and when he was absent, they acted as if he was never missed. They kept the talk flowing, which let me know they were getting along, but when I visited their group, I led the responding. Marilyn found the group pleasant, but not "helpful," which kept her from writing about important things. Karen thought the group was wonderful, got good help from the others, and revised according to their responses. David didn't seem to think he needed "help" from the others (especially since I wouldn't allow editing help) but enjoyed having an audience, and that feeling of having a live audience was powerful for him.

> *Karen:* I also really liked how we broke up into small groups. They made me feel a lot more comfortable about my writing and my responding. I'm not really sure why, but all the groups seemed to really work with each other, and I think that helped improve the writing. For me, I think the way that David and Marilyn had such different ways of interpreting what I wrote gave me more new ways to work with all of my ideas. Each paper that I worked on had many "problems" that they helped me work out. I think that the discussions we had about our lives and what was going on in the world also helped me write better. I

thought more deeply about how things affected me especially after others would seem to have the same feelings. . . .

Marilyn: I'm not the type of person who can handle a lot of criticism even if it is constructive, so I try to give my advice the way I'd want it. Because I'm so sensitive, I choose not to write about some things that I'd like to because I'm scared some one will get upset with me. That's why I didn't continue on with my "prejudice against blacks" paper. Even though I really would have liked to do some more with that, a little criticism that I got on it made me decide to put it up on the shelf. . . . I think the paper I wrote about prejudice was the most important idea I wrote about. . . . I liked my small group. We all got along well, I think. We probably didn't respond to each other's papers as well as we should have. Sometimes it seems like we'd just listen to the paper, say we liked it, and then move on to the next. Although, there were times when I had millions of new ideas for my paper after talking to my group. I felt a kind of closeness for my group. We grew to learn more about each other and I think that helped us to respond and help each other out.

David: One of the important things that has happened to me this semester is that one of my papers actually became useful. Marilyn is going to Seattle for the weekend, and the paper that I wrote about the area is serving as a tour guide. The other memorable occasion was when I wrote about midterm stress. I have never written a paper that received so much support and agreement. Everybody seemed to agree with me. The support even went so far as to have people in [my] group ask me if they could keep their copy. It felt pretty good.

Why did we get along in our group? I think that the reason was that nobody in the group tried to make themselves feel superior to anyone else. Nobody declared that they were a better writer. Every one tried to listen and help everyone else. The only problem child we had was Jeff. I don't know why he didn't come to class but I don't feel that it was because we shut him out. I personally feel that he felt so uncomfortable with his writing that he couldn't share it with us. When he did come and read what he had written, I feel that the casual response that we gave him and the casual attitude that the rest of the members of the group had developed put him off.

In terms of the collaborative small-group situation, Karen benefited the most. She worked long and hard on her paper "The Will," and she changed the paper to explain the idea to her small group. Marilyn learned about collaboration, too, but she learned that she and David couldn't collaborate on the topic she most wanted to write about. In terms of the peer-response group situation, David and Marilyn gained a better sense of audience in the sense that hearing "I like this" helps us write, but none of the group members became facilitative responders (quite consciously), which is what responding guidelines are after. They all talked about themselves as "changed" somehow (although David very little, generally revising and rewriting according to my response, rather than Marilyn's and Karen's). The two women could describe themselves as writers easily and at length in their final evaluations and describe how their writing during the semester related to those self-definitions.

The fifth role-negotiation in this group was my own as teacher. I visited this group as a fellow writer only once or twice. The first time I was able to model some helpful response by pointing out to David that one of his comments about my paper wasn't what I requested in response, because I wasn't at that particular stage in the writing process of that piece. Since I was a fellow writer, I could explain this during the small-group session, immediately after David's comment. The group as a whole could see that there were ways to respond to an overly critical remark. Most of the semester, I visited their group when they were finished reading and responding to each other's papers because they tended to finish early, before the other groups in the class. I often asked them for a report or a summary of what they were working on and what kind of response the group had given. In these oral reports, I could usually tell if the response had been too quick because of conflicts, and I drew out the rest of the story, making them, in effect, discuss again and bring out the nature of the conflict. Then I suggested other possible responses, asked why the responses conflicted, and worked out with them a way to revise.

Conflict

> [*Laura writes about her small group:*]
> As I think back to the first weeks of English I realize that we weren't really an all together group. I see now that we . . . are forming a pretty tight relationship.

> [*Kris writes:*]
> I feel that our group is made up of very different people. We all have different views on things and very different subject material. In every group session something new is learned about at least one of us.

> [*Greg writes:*]
> I think my small group was very helpful in my writing because I got to know the people and trust them as friends after the first two or three meetings with them. Once I began to trust their listening and understanding I began to write much more freely.

Diversity among group members is one the most troubling aspects of small-group work for most of our students. They come to their small group with ideas and assumptions about racial and ethnic minorities, cultural differences in communication patterns, gender biases, and certain images of themselves as members of minorities or majorities. Their affiliation with other groups is stronger than with the small group to which we assign them. Thus, to some extent, every student feels like an outsider in her group. I can't explain exactly how David, Marilyn, and Karen managed to work through their differences and find a workable, if not ideal, solution to their conflicts, a way to make each member an insider. Their experience of partial peace is not unusual, however.

As a teacher, I have fallen prey to the same problem, partly because I must anticipate or predict the needs of my students before I ever meet them, while I am planning and structuring the course. I'm sometimes held captive by similar, stereotypical assumptions about who will turn up in my classes, assumptions borne of my own cultural biases and limiting experiences: that female students have difficulty interrupting, taking leadership roles, and taking themselves seriously as students; that at-risk students have trouble with academic discourse and receive less support from family and friends to excel in school; that nontraditional, returning students are motivated and goal-oriented, have less patience for exploration and development, and have more family responsibility to balance with their schoolwork; that gay and lesbian students are completely silent about their sexuality and lifestyle in first-year classrooms, either by their own choice or due to the outright disdain and disgust expressed toward them by their fellow classmates; or that rural students are well-versed in sentence and paragraph formation, but equate editing with revision and criticizing with responding.

But those descriptions describe no individual student I have ever met. Ideally, my students' concerns with performing as students and writers should overshadow all of their differences, whether real or imagined, but I know that they don't, especially because the students' images of "student" and "writer" are culturally, experientially, and gender based. And I don't have the opportunity to understand all of the individual assumptions, attitudes, experiences, and beliefs present in my classroom before I place these individuals into groups.

Sometimes, my most pronounced cultural bias is that of teacher-thinking: I may not use the language of social interaction to describe small-group behavior as effectively as I use the language of response or critique. I often find myself talking to students at length about Peter Elbow's (1981) "movie of the mind" or Ann Berthoff's (1982) "glossing," while the students themselves are wondering why they don't like each other, why one member of their group hasn't shown up for a week, or how to tell a group member that her topic offends the group. Students tend to think about each other (and themselves) in terms of personality, tone and attitude, and commonality of goals rather than a set of communication skills.

Students tell me their group is "easy to get along with," their classmates have "honest opinions" and are "attentive and really try to help you to make a better paper." They say their small group works well when they "feel comfortable," "develop a rapport," when "nobody tries to take charge," when they can "be open with each other," and when "everyone contributes."

My goal in my classroom is to allow as many as possible of these diverse positions, experiences, and vocabularies to emerge and be in dialogue with each other. The result is conflict within the small groups in my classroom, and my students respond to this conflict in at least three ways:

1. *Withdrawal*, either from certain topics, which are consciously or unconsciously labeled "off limits," or from any serious interchange at all. Some groups are quiet because they are shy about putting themselves forward and initiating conversation, but withdrawn students or groups start out as full participants and then later refuse to enter into text-related conversation.

   For instance, a group of three young men and one young woman will often have problems if they don't have common enough interests to include the young woman in their conversations and draft material. The female member may refuse to read drafts to her small group but hand them only to her teacher for response. She may or may not remain an active responder in the group. In another case, the whole group may stop reading and responding to drafts and may even stop talking all together if they perceive that they have nothing in common or have offended each other initially by miscommunicating.

2. *Agree to disagree.* These groups will consciously say, "Well, you can believe that if you want, but I can't." As long as they also agree to take turns tolerating each other's unbelievable ideas and can treat them as unbelievable but writable, they have found a working solution to their conflicts. However, many times a small group will reach the point of agreeing to disagree and yet not be able to go any further, which allows everyone his or her "airtime" but no dialogue as a group.

3. *Work through conflicts in the roles of readers and writers.* These groups often do not acknowledge their conflicts but find ways to define their conflicts as variant interpretations or readings, confusion which requires clarification, in effect saying, "We are writers and readers with much different ideas, who want to communicate those ideas." They spend their small-group time finding ways to make those bridges and adjusting their assumptions and experiences in their texts.

Almost all groups experience all three methods of dealing with conflict; none of the three is particularly ineffective. By withdrawing from a group, a group member signals her dissatisfaction or discomfort to her teacher and the rest of her group. Some groups learn a great deal from listening to other's viewpoints without engaging in a dialogue. After listening long enough, they will often feel more confident to ask questions, and later even more confident to compare ideas and offer adjustments. And although the third method of handling conflict sounds ideal, it often backfires by assigning extremely restricted reader and writer roles.

All three methods avoid "leveling out" or moving to the "lowest common denominator" (a phenomenon administrators fear). Complete consensus is rarely a goal of any student and is never the goal of group work. Stimulating dialogue which advances each group member's understanding and opens up new perspectives, through the sharing of diverse experiences and seeking the reasons for disagreements, *is* a goal. (See Trimbur 1989 for a theoretical discussion of consensus and "dissensus" in collaboration.)

My position as authority and expert in these conflicts is (1) to provide the balance for viewpoints, by sticking up for unheard voices and making sure all students are allowed to speak fully, or by humanely forcing everyone in a small group to talk; and (2) to bring important conflicts into open discussion, often by repeating the majority and minority opinions out loud.

Supporting the minority opinion requires being present in the small group and hearing the conflict as it develops. I may say directly, "I haven't really heard why Melanie is opposed to your idea. Can you tell us more, Melanie?" Or I might simply show more interest in a difficult or poorly supported argument by saying something like, "I've heard that side from another student." Forcing each student to talk means instructing small groups in a particular agenda: "Today, I want you to take turns talking. After reading a draft, go around the circle and have each member respond before starting a give-and-take conversation."

causes more distress to the group. Treating the group as a whole as being "in conflict" or "in the process" of articulating and resolving conflict helps me, and them, identify patterns of talk and nontalk that need to be changed.

Thus, some groups who report no conflicts truly have found ways to talk around and through their disagreements and differences. Other groups reporting no conflicts, whether enjoying the group or not, are actually full of unsaid and unheard differences and misunderstandings.

Evaluating Small Groups

When so much of classroom time and energy is spent in small-group work, the small group has an enormous influence on a student's overall performance. Some students will find ways to improve their writing outside their small group if they feel their small group doesn't cooperate or help, but other students won't. Some students will attempt valiantly all semester to work with a recalcitrant or hostile group member, and others won't. Who is rewarded and who isn't? What kinds of behavior "count" and which don't? What percentage of a final course grade should include small-group work? How do I include small-group work in a portfolio grading system?

From talking to fellow teachers and from my own experience I know that these questions are often so disturbing and resistant to clear answers that they make us fearful of and annoyed by the idea of using small groups. After all, I hear myself saying, this is a writing class, not a small-group interaction class. In addition to the extra work, this need to quantify my students' behavior in addition to their written texts goes against every pedagogical belief I hold dear, but until I can persuade my department and university to eliminate the grading system, I am forced to think about small groups at some point in terms of how much, how little, how effective, how disruptive. The clearer and more concise I can be (for one semester at a time) about how a good first- or second-year college writer behaves in a small group, the more validly I can evaluate my students. One semester, in recurring attempts to describe the observable behavior of a small-group member I wrote:

> A helpful small group member actively includes everyone in the conversation, responds to texts according to instructions and the writer's requests, listens and accepts the response of other group members, asks for help, articulates problems and describes the feelings and actions of the small group, seeks to diplomatically validate differences and resolve some conflicts.

While this kind of description gives me something to base my evaluations on, it is obviously incomplete and rewards students who have had positive past small-group experiences.

Uncomfortably and precariously based on a "description," I make small-group behavior part of a "participation" grade in my class, which probably weighs in at about 20 or 25 percent of the overall final grade. If I calculated the percentage by amount of time spent or amount of influence on other gradable factors, the small-group portion ought to be around 50 percent of the students' final grade. The quality of response and support a student received in her small group effects how her revising process worked and how well her final products turned out. And because a student must be physically present to participate in her small group, attendance is a strong requirement. The response loop in a workshop-based classroom is tight enough that missing class directly effects the quality of the final product, so that deducting "points" specifically for poor attendance is hardly necessary, except as a familiar motivational device.

Therefore, I could assume that the influence of the small group, for good or ill, has indirectly affected the students' performance on informal and formal writing and doesn't need a specific portion of the grade. During other semesters, then, I don't consider small-group work as any formal part of the grade, but when finalizing course grades, I will give the generous benefit of the doubt to members of small groups who made specific, memorable contributions to their small groups.

Based on my individual concept of fairness, I can't give "group grades." The dynamics of interpersonal relationships are too tenuous, fluid, and unpredictable to make valid evaluations of "how well" a group works together. A student could fit my evaluative description of a helpful small-group member but meet with constant and strong opposition to her every effort. I may not understand or see that a student is making this kind of effort because I am focusing on the reactions of other members. Many small groups are fraught with difficulties and yet learn a great deal about writing and produce well-crafted texts. Other small groups can work independently and effectively and still not offer any proof of learning. The most influential talk of a small group may happen when I am not participating in the group, which pulls the real work of small groups even farther from my evaluative eye.

The only aspect of small-group work which I am comfortable evaluating is the progression of articulate self-reports of small-group influence on a student's writing process and written texts. In order to do this, I must have a series of written reports during the semester in which students explain to me what's happening in their small groups, sometimes freely generated and sometimes in response to specific questions from me. These written reports are included in the students' portfolios as part of end-of-semester letters to me about their thinking, writing, and learning. If I assign collaborative writing, where two or more students generate one text, each student receives a grade based on his or her written reports to me about how the collaboration worked and didn't work, not on the text itself. The reliance on the "stability" of written texts, whether formal or informal, self-directed or audience-directed, is probably a disadvantage as much as an advantage of my grading system, and I try to remember to keep notes on oral reports from students and the time I spend in small groups observing and participating.

Conclusions

Evaluation is probably the worst note on which to conclude a chapter on small groups. I'm not sure that performance in small groups necessarily needs to be a part of a teacher's evaluation process at all, especially if it will keep a teacher from experimenting and revising her ideas on small groups. In fact, the most useful invitations to a writer's life from this chapter are not likely to come from the specific techniques or models of small groups that I described, but from the mental activities that will keep us thinking and advancing our knowledge and understanding:

- imagining a personal vision of a perfect small group or class of small groups;
- remembering our own small-group experiences;
- comparing students' versions of effective interaction with our own versions;
- contrasting stories of small groups with other instructors; and
- becoming members of small groups in class and outside of class.

Notes

1. While research in other fields has contributed to our understanding of small groups, it tends to look for ways to define, divide, categorize, and explain away much of what we would define as the rich textures of small-group behavior. One of my very favorite studies is Gemmill and Wynkoop (1991), in which four "transformational phases" are defined in groups that meet for some form of self-analysis leading to increased self-knowledge. The article includes

some dramatic diagrams of the "vortexes of chaos" and roller coaster movements of small groups as they organize themselves. Another example is Fisher's (1980) textbook for speech communication courses, in which small groups become "coherent" through the plotting on graphs of certain characteristics while ignoring others.

2. The composition classes I am describing are variations on the required curriculum for first-year composition at the University of Nebraska–Lincoln and Florida State University. The curriculum is a two-semester sequence, loosely organized around the development of individual writing facility and expanded practice and experience with writing texts and responding to other writers, from writing within one's experience during the first semester to writing from other sources of information and interpretation during the second. Both semesters emphasize ways to handle various writing processes, invention (especially discovering the topics of one's own authority), and revision. Portfolio and holistic evaluation, small-group work, and an informally published collection of class essays are often part of the course structure. Students write and revise several essays, keep a journal or writer's notebook, write extensively during class, and meet with their instructor for individual conferences.

Within those guidelines, instructors may give assignments or allow students to choose their topics. Instructors decide for themselves how much time to spend on invention, revision, and response; choose readings to supplement class work; and may or may not deal with mechanical issues or assign library research during either semester.

5 Individualization and Group Work: A Small-Group Writing Workshop and Individualized Invitations to a Writer's Life

Robert Brooke
University of Nebraska–Lincoln

For the first time in years, I am excited about writing. At the beginning of the semester when you talked to us about our major goal being to live the life of a writer, I was confused and apprehensive. I get it now. I'm dealing with topic choices that I didn't have the courage to do before. "Ike" and "The Black Boots" are excellent examples. My personal motivation has been to sort out my feelings on these subjects and to convey them to a reader. Growth in this area includes the topic choices themselves, being true, and evolving from this-is-how-it-happened to "What if?" I'm a lot braver now and am proud of much of what I have done in this class—even though I didn't get "Ike" done. If anything, stopping with what I wrote appeals to me more than forcing the ending at this time. Deadlines are valid, but I can't rush the Creator. I feel like a writer now—one who is just beginning to really get to know herself in this way. Therefore, although this class is over, "Ike" is not. (Can I bring him in when I think I've got it in the final stages??) I'm not a writer "wanna be" anymore.

> —Excerpt from a student's final
> portfolio letter

One poem or story doesn't matter one way or the other. It's the process of writing and life that matters.

> —Natalie Goldberg, *Writing Down
> the Bones* (1986)

In my classes, small groups are an integral part of the invitation to a writer's life that I try to create for my students. Small groups are necessary in order to surround developing writers with the community context, response, and exposure that can help them visualize how writing might be useful throughout their lives. Small groups provide the social context in which individual students can see and imagine themselves as writers. But what guides my classes aren't primarily the small groups: rather, it's the individual invitation to a writer's life that I extend to each student.

Since each person's life is different, the way the practice of writing will fit into each life is also different. The practice of writing varies from individual to individual, as shown by students from my class last semester:

- Shannon, a sprinter in her final year of school after five years of competitive collegiate athletics, journaled regularly about her upcoming life choices, her relationships with friends still in track, and her feelings about being a minority student in a predominantly white midwestern city. Since she'd never imagined herself as a writer before (having used academic tutors to complete her assigned school papers) and didn't imagine herself going on in school after graduation, she told me she didn't see the point of public writing such as essays or editorials for her immediate future. But she did say that writing daily and then discussing her ideas with others prompted her to believe that writing can be an aid to her own decision making.

- Doug, a pre-med student in his junior year, told me he's an avid reader of writers like Lewis Thomas and Richard Seltzer, and believed that writing those sorts of essays about professional and personal experience was something he'd like to do. In class, he began writing about his stormy relationship with his father and became more and more interested in the goal of publishing this essay in a literary journal (and perhaps continuing to write such essays as an ongoing sideline to his medical studies).

- Elizabeth, a sophomore psychology major who wanted to go to graduate school, devoted her semester to developing a research proposal for a possible undergraduate thesis on Alzheimer's treatment and explained that she was purposefully exploring the kind of writing she imagines doing for her life's work.

- Jed, a sophomore criminal justice major taking a required writing course, found himself writing a new kind of piece every week, from long-overdue letters to his mother in western Nebraska, to a love poem to his girlfriend, to a series of incident reports like those he imagines real police officers have to write. As he tried out these writings, he wrote to me privately saying that he avoided reading this material in group because it was too embarrassing, but that he enjoyed more than anything else hearing all his classmates' writing. He mused that his audiences may be the people he writes his pieces for, not his group, but then also asked my advice after the semester was over for what other courses to take for an English minor with a concentration in writing.

As these quick sketches make clear, students find unique ways of fitting writing into the myriad lives they lead, and consequently, the invitation to a writer's life, even when offered to a class full of people who will be working in the presence of one another for a semester or longer, is actually better thought of as a set of loosely linked individual invitations.

An invitation to a writer's life asks students to explore writing in the context of their lives to see where its rhythms fit. To enable this exploration to take place, my classroom strives to provide two ongoing sets of activities. First, my classroom promotes writerly behaviors, especially regular writing, reading, and discussion of writing. Second, my classroom promotes continuing reflection on the personal significance of these behaviors. Writerly behaviors are important because they give developing writers the experiential base from which to arrive at their own conclusions about the place of writing in their lives. But without ongoing reflection on the significance of those behaviors in the context of individual lives, such conclusions are likely to be lost amid the pressures of the college routine.

Small groups are an essential element of the invitation to a writer's life that I offer. Groups provide opportunities to respond to and share writing, as well as exposure to the various kinds of writing different people find important. And reflection on group interactions helps developing writers articulate the significance of writerly experiences for themselves and others.

In this chapter, I'll describe how I set up my writing classes to provide writerly behavior and reflection for my students, emphasizing the place of small-group work as a support for these necessities. I'll begin by sketching the general way I organize my courses to provide writerly behavior and reflection, and then I'll describe the ways I use small groups within this structure.

Predictable Activities, Goal Setting, and Portfolio Evaluation: The Rhythms of a Writing Workshop

Because my overall goal in my classes is to encourage students to explore a writer's life as a supporting element in the lives they lead, I need to provide my students with a structure in which they can determine for themselves what's essential about the practice of writing. As developing writers, my students need to identify those aspects of writing which seem most beneficial to them, to explore and experiment with those aspects, and to come to some initial judgments about how best to fit those aspects of writing into their future lives. In short, my students need a structure in which they have enough personal control over their work to set their own goals for writing and to explore the consequences of those choices—but they also need a structure which exposes them to aspects of a writer's life they might not think of on their own.

Over the past few semesters, I've been exploring a structure for writing classes that emphasizes predictable activities, goal setting, and portfolio evaluation. I've arrived at this structure largely because it seems to provide students with the self-control and the exposure to new aspects of writing which I think they need.

For me as a teacher, arriving at this structure has required that I give up some of my earlier ideas about my role as teacher. When I first started teaching, I thought my role as teacher meant that I had to make sequences of assignments for students to progress through, hopefully with each successive assignment requiring the mastery of a new rhetorical strategy. So I organized my syllabi and my classes around the assignments I would give. It took me several years of such teaching to realize that my sequences of assignments worked against any real invitation to a writer's life: they kept me, as teacher, in charge of the writing, and my students off balance. They could only guess which assignment would come next, and hence they couldn't plan their future work. I, not they, chose the purpose for their writing because all of my sequences had the goal of mastering rhetorical strategies. I, not they, established how much time their writing would take, based on how long of a piece I required each week. Over time, I slowly came to realize that my sequences of assignments inhibited my students from really imagining themselves as people who use writing in their lives, and so I had to give up that way of structuring my classes (see Brooke 1991, which describes this shift in my teaching in greater detail).

I now try hard not to structure my classes around sequences of assignments that I plan and my students can only guess at. In fact, I try not to use assignments at all. I no longer assign topics, purposes, genres, or rhetorical problems to my students to guide their writing. Instead, my syllabi list requirements they must fulfill to complete the course successfully: doing a minimum of six hours of writing each week out of class; bringing a new or substantially revised piece of writing to small-group meetings each week; attending and being prepared for all class sessions; submitting portfolios of their collected work in the fifth, tenth, and final weeks of the semester. And my syllabi also explain the predictable weekly organization of the course. I have, in short, moved from a syllabus structured around sequenced assignments I create to one structured around repeated, predictable activities which students can use to accomplish their own writing projects.

Predictable Activities

From the very first week of school, I establish predictable routines in my classroom: on Tuesdays, we work with an activity to help with one of the major tasks writers face (invention, organization, revision, editing), and we have some kind of discussion of the reading we've done; on Thursdays, we meet to share drafts of our own work in small groups, and then we write and discuss reflections on the week's writing and class work. Every Thursday (in a first-year class) and every other Thursday (in sophomore- and junior-level classes), students also give me some material they want me to read and comment on—perhaps a piece they've drafted that they want a specific response to, perhaps some questions about writing that came up in their process logs, or perhaps a note about a problem they're having and need help with. While the individual writing activities or group work may vary, this overall pattern for class time doesn't. Because this tempo to our class time remains the same, within a few weeks students can begin to plan their writing around these activities, functionally setting up their own goals for what to explore and accomplish within these weekly rhythms.

I'll describe the Thursday small groups in the second half of this chapter, but let me say a bit more here about the Tuesday writing activities. In these Tuesday activities, I try to give my students what's functionally a smorgasbord of strategies they can try for working directly on the major problems all writers face: coming up with topics and ideas, finding or making a workable organization for those ideas, identifying and completing revision for content and organization, and editing. In deciding what strategies to present to a given class, I draw from my own writing experience, from what I know of these particular students, and from my reading of the professional literature. Early in the semester, before I know much about my students, I usually present activities that I personally rely on in developing ideas for my own writing. I assume, for better or worse, that many of them will be struggling to identify topics that hold their interest and hence can use invention strategies. I also assume that I can best model the behavior of an adult practicing writer by drawing directly on my own practice. As the semester progresses, though, I will tend to bring in activities that address particular problems people in class are facing. If a set of students are having trouble imagining enough material to write about, I'll present some activities in class that help writers generate material: such activities might include freewriting, clustering, tagmemics, and guided invention. If some are having trouble imagining readers who might care about their work beyond this class, I might present some audience analysis techniques in class: such as Aristotelian categories for purpose or Young, Becker, and Pike's lists of possible changes writers can effect in a reader's worldview. If others are having trouble seeing where revision for content is needed in their writing, I'll present some describing or close reading strategies for identifying what's actually there in a text: such as Berthoff's interpretive paraphrase or Flower's issue trees and "What I really mean is. . . . " My goal, as much as possible, is to try to match the activities to the present needs of at least some of my students. Since students will of course be at different places in their writing at different times in the semester, there can never be a complete match between a particular strategy and the needs of the whole class—which is why these strategies need to be presented as a smorgasbord from which developing writers can choose rather than as something they must try.

In presenting these activities, I try generally to work from three principles: (1) *keep it real*—that is, keep the activity in the context of our own writing, not of examples from other sources, and do the activity myself with my students on a piece I am currently writing; (2) *provide time*—give ample time to sample the activity in class; and (3) *provide reflection*—give ample time for individuals to report how the activity worked, so that the range of how this activity affects different people can be part of class. These principles suggest a fairly predictable way of conducting Tuesday activities: I tend to start with a short description of which writer's problem the activity can help with, and then divide the activity into two or three steps which we work through in order, pausing for volunteers to read aloud what they've produced and to discuss what happened at the end of each step. This way of doing activities leads to a predictable procedure of three ten-minute activity steps followed by five-minute discussions during any single class period.

Goal Setting

The predictable nature of the class activities makes goal setting possible. Because students know what's likely to be coming up in class, they can plan ahead what they want to work on, choosing both which topics or genres they might want to explore as well as which strategies they might like to try for overcoming their particular writing blocks. Starting in the second week of the semester, I ask students to develop some short-term goals for their writing and some strategies they'd like to try as a means of achieving these goals. (To help them develop goals that will be useful for them, I will often guide them through an inventory of their own writing processes during Tuesday's writing activity in the second week.) Because of the importance of regular writing time in a writer's life, I insist that one of these goals be a time-management goal that sets aside a substantial chunk of time each week for their writing (I suggest six hours per week as a basic minimum). The other goals they choose themselves, based on their own sense of what they need and want to work on in their writing. I schedule individual conferences with each student during the second week of classes to discuss these goals with them, to help them clarify what they want to accomplish, and to suggest strategies for achieving their goals when they aren't sure what to try. After these conferences, I make up a handout for class of all these individual goals, which I distribute so that everyone in class gets exposure to the kinds of writing issues other individuals in class are addressing. Here's a representative sample of such goals in the second week of school, from my sophomore/junior-level writing course in fall 1992:

> *Bill:* I suffer procrastination and pressure blocks, tending only to write when outside pressure makes me, and the block appears as I try to find my topic. So to start with I'll try to make this block work for me by assigning myself a new piece of writing three times a week, and writing a good draft in two hours. I'll generally use Monday, Wednesday, and Sunday for these writing times. Robert has assigned me topics for two of these many writings: the block itself, and why I want to go to law school.

> *June:* My goals are working with personal style to make it more universal and expanding writing beyond a page or two. To manage this, I'll try writing first for myself on what's most important to me for three hours in a journal, then making a choice whether to develop that or something else for group. I'll keep track of time with start/stop times in margins.

> *Susan:* I've been writing in the sciences for four years and I want to write something entirely different to develop wider scope. I'd most like to try fiction because that's what I enjoy reading. I'll try cut and paste and loop writing as ways to start. Time goal: I'll record start and stop times for my writing in the margins of my notebook, aiming for 6 hours per week.

> *Elizabeth:* I'll write for a while on past experiences and the uncertainty of life after graduation, then in a few weeks I'll work on a proposal for volunteer work, applications for graduate school, and maybe term papers in psych if I can arrange it with my instructors. I'll try fitting writing hours in after work, an hour after I get off each day.

Doug: I want to do journal writing for myself. I've been doing daily writing at the end of my day most days. I have a secondary goal to move towards publishable writing, and may explore that.

Shannon: To meet the time requirement, I'll write in the margin when I start and stop, aiming for 6 hours. I want to start with personal things and opinions, because that's the easiest for me.

At the second week of the semester, these lists of goals show a huge range in students' awareness of themselves as writers and in their ability to monitor their own writing practice. Some students, like Bill and June, are highly aware of the blocks they suffer (for Bill, it's procrastination; for June, it's self-editing to the extent that she can't write more than two pages on anything), but they are unsure of what to try to overcome these blocks. In my goal-setting conference with these students, I often suggest a range of strategies they can try to combat these blocks. From this discussion, they choose a few strategies to try right away (Bill opts for making his existing process a virtue rather than a vice by purposefully overdoing it; June opts to separate personal and public writing into distinct stages). Other students, like Susan and Elizabeth, have a clear sense of what they'd like to write (fiction for Susan; self-reflection and term papers for Elizabeth), but they don't feel they suffer any particular blocks in writing. In my goal-setting conferences with these students, I usually explore with them their awareness of their writing processes. When, as was the case with Susan and Elizabeth, they can describe their writing processes and don't perceive any trouble with writing, we simply use the topic and time goals for their writing. Still other students, like Doug and Shannon, aren't at all sure what they want to write and seem to feel a bit lost with the process of goal setting itself. With such students, the goal-setting conference often becomes a chance to talk about the various ways in which people use writing in their lives (from personal journal writing, to public debate in editorials, to attempts to work out ideas or persuade others in essays), and almost universally such students choose to begin by keeping a personal journal.

There are three overriding purposes behind these goals conferences: (1) to help students begin taking control over their own writing by setting short-term goals; (2) to help them begin monitoring their own writing processes self-consciously; and (3) to meet individually with each student so that we can work out privately any confusion the student may have about class structure. As the semester progresses, students have the opportunity to reflect on their short-term goals three times, and set new ones as their needs change.

Portfolio Evaluation

The goals students set in week two guide their work roughly for three weeks, until their first portfolio is due in week five. After they have received their portfolio evaluations in week six, we meet again in goals conferences to set new goals for the second five weeks of the course. In week ten, they again submit portfolios, and in week eleven they establish a final set of goals for the last five weeks of the semester. In short, the semester proceeds through three five-week periods, during each of which students set new goals and compile a portfolio of their work for evaluation. After the first five-week period, this schedule becomes as predictable for students as the other elements of the course, thereby allowing them to plan for evaluation and goal setting as well as for Tuesday activities and Thursday group days.

In week five, the first portfolio is submitted to me for evaluation, and contains three main parts: (1) The portfolio begins with a letter to me describing their experience so far in the course, with special attention to how their work demonstrates their completion of the course requirements and their own goals. (2) The portfolio then presents an annotated table of contents which organizes their work so far into chunks they can describe. (If a student has worked on three papers, for example, and written several drafts of each, she might organize her work around these three papers. If, by contrast, a student has rarely worked on the same subject when he wrote but has instead tried out a variety of different pieces, he might organize his work around categories like "Writing from Class Activities," "Private Journals," and "Pieces for Group." Some students arrange their work around the goals they've set themselves, producing a table of contents like June's first portfolio, which had sections on "Writing with my internal editor turned off," "Writing before we had our goals conference," and "Drafts of my 'Ike' paper for small group.") (3) The portfolio then gathers their work for the first five weeks into the categories they've formed in the table of contents.

I read these portfolios over the weekend and write an evaluation letter to each student, in which I comment on (a) their work as a citizen in the class community (that is, on matters like meeting deadlines and having writing for their groups); (b) the growth I see in their writing process; and (c) the quality of their finished writing. Usually, in writing these comments I am repeating or commenting on things they say about themselves in the portfolio letters. I then offer the student some advice for the next section of the course and assign a single overall grade for the work as a whole.

After returning the portfolios and evaluations in class on Tuesday of week six, I schedule a second round of goals conferences at the end of the week. In this second round of conferences, we try to refine each person's goals in light of their first five week's work and set new goals which will help them with what now seems most important. As teacher, I also learn from the portfolio letters and goals conferences what kinds of activities I should plan during the second five weeks of class.

Here's an example of how this portfolio process works. Deb entered my fall 1992 sophomore/junior-level writing class as a junior social services major with three year's experience working with leadership programs on campus. During our first goals conference in week two, she expressed a good deal of confidence in her writing, told me how much she admired Robert Fulghum's recent books *All I Really Needed to Know I Learned in Kindergarten* (1988) and *It Was on Fire When I Lay Down on It* (1989), and proposed to try writing a series of pieces like his, based on her own life. For her goal statement, she described her goals in this way:

> I will write about feelings and opinions, but not directly so much as through analogy, comparison, extension, like in Robert Fulghum's writing. I'll also do some private personal writing—letters that I'll never send. I'll mark start and stop times in margins to monitor writing hours.

In the three weeks preceding the submission of her first portfolio, Deb attended class all but one day and participated fully in writing and group activities. In weeks two and four, she handed in to me for comment sets of papers she'd written which did indeed try out comparisons as a means of writing about her own life. In week two, she handed in a piece comparing her life in college to that of a baby bird being pushed out of a nest, a piece reflecting on the natural beauty she sees in a sunset, and a paper about the positive effects of smiling when life treats you poorly. In week four, she turned in a prose poem written from the point of view of a tree watching the growth of a younger tree (which she said in her process log was about her and her brother) and a revision of her piece on parents and the bird being pushed from the nest. As anyone who has read *All I Really Needed to Know I Learned in Kindergarten* will immediately recognize, the topics Deb chose and her organizational strategies do resemble the pieces in Fulghum's books of inspirational writing. From what I could see, Deb was indeed working on her goal of writing like Fulghum, and was finding the folksy sorts of analogies he often uses to make his points. But from what I could see,

I also worried that Deb's analogies might sometimes be too restrictive for her ideas, a bit facile, rather than allowing her to find the sorts of new insights that make Fulghum's best prose exciting.

Since Deb had turned in more than one piece each time work was due, I assumed I had seen most of her writing for the four weeks and was consequently fretting about how I would respond to her work when her portfolio was submitted. I worried about my role as evaluator—I wanted to reward her for the clear way in which she'd explored the organizational strategies of her favorite author, but I also wanted to push her to try for some fresher analogies that would open up her imagination rather than restrict it.

With these worries in mind, I was pleased to discover what was actually in her portfolio. Her portfolio contained forty pages of writing, of which I had seen approximately half. She divided her table of contents into two sections, "all work previously handed in" and "some copies of rough drafts." The "previous work" section listed the five pieces I had seen, with the following note appended:

> I have worked on my parents analogy the most this semester, but feel it needs to be put away for a while. I am now going back to work on My Baby Brother, and have a few ideas I want to play with. This is a perfect example of two essays I have been trying to define.

The "copies of rough drafts" section read as follows:

1. Scott's accident, a page of notes
2. Unknown Nightmare, rough draft
3. Unknown Nightmare, second copy

> This was taking a totally different approach than what I was used to, but I wanted to get something out of it. I have been trying for a long time to express this on paper and this poem has been the closest thing.

4. Through the Years

> This writing is one that needs to be revised, and I want to work with it more. It is more of the freewriting I was talking about.

5. Moodiness
6. Relationships

> Both are examples of journal writings

7. Family

> This was the rough draft to both my analogies: My Baby Brother and My Parents analogy. Both of them also need to be defined more clearly.

8. Marriage and My Best Friend

9. I'm Me
10. Grandpa

These are all thoughts I have had but never expressed. I don't know where they are going from here. They will probably sit for a while.

Clearly, Deb had been doing more work than what she'd submitted to me already, and her notes about the pieces (such as "This is a perfect example of two essays I have been trying to define") hinted that she was engaged in more complex thinking about her subjects than her pieces could so far show.

Her letter to me about her work for the course put her submitted pieces into a larger context: that of someone finding that writing often helps you discover more than you initially had thought was there. Deb wrote:

My writing has started out as a type of journal, which wasn't what I had planned. I found myself expressing my daily frustrations, joys, or any other mood I was in. At first, this in itself was frustrating in that I wanted to jump into writing like Robert Fulghum's. My first paper came easily and I thought I could continue this without any problems. I knew I had a lot I could write about, but once I got started with different analogies, "feelings" got in the way. When I say got in the way, I mean I was confused with what I wanted to say because I never really sat down to think how I felt on these issues.

Later in her letter, she continued this idea:

I have found that it has taken a lot more time and effort to really get to the heart of what I am trying to express. Throughout my journals I get a spark of what I want to write about, but only once in a while. . . . My new goal as a writer is to take a step back. . . . I want to work on revisions and being able to locate "hearts" of the paper to again free write on a more narrow topic. I sometimes feel I have to type out a masterpiece when I write. This has prevented me from understanding what I could actually possess and get out of my writing. I think taking a step back and beginning from there might actually help me see through this.

In the last section of her letter, Deb asked for two kinds of help in the upcoming weeks of class. First, she wanted to have her group members take her writing home and write on it some honest reactions about what they liked and what they wanted changed. Second, she wanted me to lead the class in more revision activities, especially ones that would help her clarify her ideas.

Deb, in short, described in her portfolio exactly the worry I'd had about her writing—she, too, felt that her initial drafts weren't fully exploring her topics, and maybe weren't even emphasizing what was most important. But her portfolio also showed that these problems existed in the context of on ongoing struggle to determine exactly what was at the heart of her—a struggle that prompted her to identify some problems with focus (where at the beginning of the course she didn't perceive any problems at all) and a shifting purpose to her writing. As she described it:

> I have always tried to write for other people, never for myself. I think this has been one of my biggest problems as I started this course. I thought of writing as an entertainment profession, but writing my journals has helped me otherwise. I have been in writing classes for four years and I am just now realizing what it is all about.

After reading Deb's letter, table of contents, and portfolio, I felt much more confident in my role of evaluator of her work. As often happens when I read portfolios, I discovered that Deb was already aware of the things that bothered me in her writing and in fact had already begun to form some plans for overcoming these problems. I also discovered that Deb's writing occurred in a context of much richer thinking about writing than I'd suspected, freeing me as teacher to respond to that context of richer thinking as well as responding to the writing itself.

Here's the evaluation letter I wrote Deb at the beginning of week six:

> Deb—
> Here's how your work for the first five weeks looks to me:
> *Citizenship:* You've had perfect, on-time attendance except for the Thursday after Labor Day, but you got me your work for that week anyway. You participate well in small group and full class. Overall, near perfect for this part of class.
> *Growth in Process:* As you say in your letter to me, your process is surprising you some because it's going in a direction you didn't expect. Where you'd expected to be writing directly for your readers in analogy pieces, you are finding you get more out of journaling first as a means of more thoroughly exploring your ideas/feelings on the material. I think this is true about your work. The combined work on your brother is the clearest example. I don't know in what order you wrote the journals and the tree piece, but I see the two supporting each other, needing to grow together. I find myself wanting to suggest that you use journals as freewriting to develop ideas, your more public writing as places for trying to shape those ideas so chosen others can benefit from them, and process logs as the way to let your mind build the bridges between the two. Looks to me like the process you're developing is working well.
> *Quality of Writing:* Given the detour you are finding yourself taking in the journal writing, I think the quality of your pieces is what we can reasonably expect at this point. What you have are

pieces in which a good, solid idea appears, and now you are working to develop the potential of those ideas into something that teaches your readers what you want them to learn. At present, I sense you are yourself learning from your pieces and are midpotential with them. They are a notch beyond first drafts, but you don't yet have full control over them. I think this is about all we can expect at week five.

Advice: Adapt your goals to make journaling, writing on pieces, and process logs support each other in your work. This may require an increase in time. Basically, take the advice you are giving yourself. I think it will work.

Overall Grade: A.

—Robert

During our goals conference in the week following this portfolio submission, Deb talked more about her feeling of writing around the "heart" of what she was writing, and explained that she felt she could see the "heart" of the piece better at a distance of several days than right away. She came up with the following goals statement for the next five weeks:

Continue writing journals nightly. Then work on revisions. One week later, I want to reread journals and consider developing a piece from them. Need help grasping revision. Time is fine; journaling makes this easier.

In going through the portfolio process, Deb had functionally identified for herself something she wanted to improve in her writing, a way of describing what that thing was, and a strategy for such improvement. She was also able to ask my help in designing class activities which would assist her in clarifying her central points and seeing where in her texts these points appeared most forcefully. In a complementary fashion, the portfolio process stopped me from responding to the wrong features of Deb's work. Because I was able to see her writing in the context of her thinking and all her work for the first five weeks, I responded to that context rather than to the features of her texts which most bothered me when it came time to evaluate. The process also showed me what I needed to plan for Tuesday activities to help Deb and the three or four students like her, and in the eighth week of this class I had us work with interpretive paraphrase as a means of seeing what is actually in our texts instead of what we merely hope is there.

Workshop Rhythms and Control

The main reason I now organize my writing classes around predictable activities, goal setting, and portfolio evaluation is that this organization provides students with greater control over their learning. By the time we've finished the first five weeks of class, they know what to expect for the remaining ten: they've done a lot of Tuesday writing activities and Thursday groups; they've set goals and reconsidered them; they've put together a portfolio, experiencing both how they themselves make sense of their work and how I evaluate it. Since they know what to expect, they can begin to plan how they will use this structure for their own ends. And that, finally, is my overarching goal. I want my students to have the opportunity to plan how writing can fit into their lives, to explore what its rhythms can contribute. At the end of the term, I want my students to be able to make informed choices about writing's place in their lives. For this to happen, they need some personal control over the ways in which they use writing, and some personal control is what this kind of classroom structure provides.

Establishing Procedures, Monitoring Interaction, Experiencing Diversity: Groups in Writing Workshops

For me, small groups help achieve the goal of providing students with the personal control necessary to make informed choices about the place of writing in their lives. Group discussions of writing expose students to a variety of responses to their own writing, to a sampling of the diverse purposes others have for their writing, and to some of the many ways other people manage their own writing processes. Since the people in these groups come from the full range of people who now take classes in higher education, the exposure to writing that students receive in groups is both more complex and more closely tied to the varieties of life than what they can receive from any single writing teacher's responses. In short, groups provide, directly and vicariously, many of the writing experiences that students will need to make truly informed choices about the future roles writing might play in their own lives. Groups create the social context in which individuals can identify and explore the writer's roles that seem most appealing to them.

As with the Tuesday writing activities in my class, the Thursday small-group meetings are both social interactions and individual invitations to a writer's life. They provide writerly behaviors and opportunities for reflection. Where Tuesday writing activities engage students in some of the mental strategies and problems that writers encounter whenever they write, the Thursday group meetings engage students in response to particular texts and discussion of group members' purposes and processes for writing. Where reflecting on Tuesday activities helps students identify and explore the strategies available to them as they write, reflecting on Thursday small groups helps them identify and explore the range of purposes and uses for writing that exist within our culture. Together, the writing activities and the small groups surround students with the essential writerly behaviors and reflections they need to identify their own future uses of writing.

Although groups provide much of the social interaction necessary to understand what's possible in writing, it is the individual person who needs finally to make informed choices about her own uses of writing. Groups are social. They can be collaborative, supportive, argumentative, soul-searching, or apathetic, but it is the unique way each individual makes sense of what occurs in the group that determines how that person will use the writing discussed there. It's the individual's response to the social interaction that informs her later choices, not just the interaction itself. In my classes, the group work students engage in is certainly the most important part of their classroom experience, but it occurs within a structure of individually set goals for writing and individually compiled portfolios which both record and reflect on the student's own exploration of writing. The group meetings are the site for the most important and productive work of my writing classes, but the work itself is individual.

This principle of the dual nature of groups (as both social and individual) has led me to realize over and over again that the real work of groups is the student's own—and not in my control as teacher. Developing writers make their own sense of the responses they get in groups and the interactions that occur there, and that's what determines their learning. Because of the individual nature of this learning, my role toward the groups can't be that of a controlling teacher who dictates how everything must occur. I just can't control how individuals will respond to what happens, even if I could control how groups talk to each other. Instead, I can only tell my students the things I believe are crucial about groups for writers, and then work with my students as individuals while they negotiate their own ways through the complex realities of group interaction.

Consequently, group work in my classes has evolved over time into a pattern which emphasizes the individual's responsibility for the significance of group interaction. I first tell my students collectively why I believe group experience is crucial for writers and what I think characterizes the most effective group interaction, then let my students engage in group work with little intervention from me, and finally help my students as individuals to reflect on what their group experience means for them. By and large, they design their own interventions in their groups. This pattern guides all aspects of group work, from how groups are established in my classroom to the ways groups handle and complete their work.

Establishing Group Procedures

My overall goal for the small groups in my classes is for the individual students to come to realize what they need from others to support their writing. I want them to leave at the end of the semester with a sense of the people with whom they enjoy talking about writing, the responses they find most helpful for their writing, and the things they can do to create their particular kind of supportive writing group now that class is over. Consequently, in establishing and managing group procedures, I require that my students become active participants in choosing who is in their group and how that group functions. Such active involvement in managing the group means that students must think about the way the group works. Whether a group has succeeded or failed in meeting a given student's needs, that student leaves the class understanding that she has choices concerning the responses and people with whom she surrounds her writing, and that those choices have consequences.

I set only three fixed requirements for groups. (1) Groups meet every Thursday for about fifty minutes of the seventy-five-minute class period, and attendance is required. (2) Everyone (including me) is required to bring a substantially new piece of writing to each group meeting. (Substantially new writing includes significant revisions of old pieces, continuations of ongoing pieces, and shifts from one genre to another—say, from prose description to poetry—as well as brand new pieces.) Each person should bring enough photocopies of the piece so that each group member has one unless there's a good reason for not to copying the work (good reasons might include the piece containing highly personal material or the writer wanting an aural rather than visual response to the piece). (3) After the group discussion (either in class, if there's time, or sometime later that same day), each person is required to write a response to the group meeting, in which he or she addresses three questions: "What happened?" "What do I think of my piece now?" and "What will I try next?" (I've adapted these questions from Elbow and Belanoff 1989). These responses, which I call "process logs" (following Elbow and Belanoff), become part of each student's portfolio at the fifth, tenth, and final weeks of the semester.

These three requirements dictate that all students come to groups with new writing to share and that they reflect on the group experience after it's over. When students miss a group day, don't have writing, or don't complete their process logs, they and their group know they are misbehaving in the context of the class, and after the first portfolio in week five, they know as well that such behavior affects directly the citizenship portion of their grade.

Beyond these three requirements, however, what I offer my students are suggestions for group interaction and aids for individually understanding and improving their group behavior, especially in the two crucial areas of forming groups and developing discussion strategies that meet their needs.

1. Forming Groups

My suggestions start with the formation of the groups themselves. While my goal is to have the class form groups of four to five people which will remain the same for the duration of the semester, I begin the class with a period of experimentation. For the first three weeks, I encourage students to get into Thursday groups with different people each week and to record thoroughly their impressions of these groups afterward. Then, as part of Tuesday's class in week four, I ask each student to make three lists: one list of the four to six people she absolutely wants to have in her group, a second list of up to four people she wouldn't mind being with in a group, and a final list of individuals she does not want in her group under any circumstances. By Thursday, I collate these lists into groups based on the students' choices, and the resulting groups usually remain the same for the duration of the semester.

I've learned through experience that these lists need to be written out privately—it doesn't work as well to have students just break into groups on the fourth Tuesday because of Nebraska students' unwillingness to be impolite to each other. When they can write the lists out privately, they can exclude students they'd rather not work with, something they can't do in the free-for-all of a class group-formation time.

For example, in last fall's sophomore/junior-level writing class, Doug wrote to me privately on his list that he didn't want to be in a group with a certain student because they had previously been boyfriend and girlfriend, and as a result, he felt unable to be fully honest around her. This other student had purposefully put herself in Doug's group during each of the three experimental weeks and had put him on her "top choice" list. Without the possibility of Doug informing me privately of the difficulty of this situation, they would have ended up in a group together, and I doubt whether Doug would have then felt able to write as searchingly about his father as he did.

By contrast, two years ago, when I was first experimenting with letting students form their own groups, I had students just form groups in class without private lists. By week five, several groups were having problems, most often because of the conflicts between out-of-class friendships and in-class response to writing. One group of four women exemplified these problems. Two of the students wrote privately in their process logs that all four of them had been close friends for several years, that they had chosen to work together because one of these friends suggested they should, and that they didn't want to betray their friendship by choosing another group. The problem was that the two most talkative group members spent far too much time talking about their own papers and out-of-class activities, so that the other two students rarely had a chance to discuss their writing. These latter two were frustrated, feeling profoundly the conflict between their close personal friendship, on the one hand, and their desire for better response to their writing, on the other. Since many of the groups in this class were facing similar problems, I had the whole class change groups at midterm, using private lists of who they'd like to have in their groups. (Peg and Roger, the two students I reported on in chapter 2, were students in this class, and their reports show how much better the second groups were for them.) Experiences like these have convinced me that students need the opportunity to tell me privately and confidentially of their group preferences if I want their own choices of groups to be a positive feature of group interaction.

Experiences like these have also led to the advice I give students about group formation. During the three-week period of experimentation, and then again on the day they make their lists of potential group members, I usually put on the board something like the following:

> *The best writing groups have the following characteristics:*
>
> 1. They include people you respect, but not necessarily people to whom you are responsible in other ways (that is, childhood friends, roommates, family members, and people you are dating often make poor group members).
>
> 2. They include people who are different enough from you that they will give you fresh perspectives, but not people who are so different that you are likely to feel antagonistic toward them.
>
> 3. The mix of people should not isolate any individual as the-only-one- of-that-kind-of-person (that is, groups shouldn't include three devout Christians and one atheist, or three men and one woman, or three anything and one different). If you do form a group of this sort, be forewarned that the single person will have to work harder not to feel isolated, and the others will have to work harder not to isolate that person.

4. For a fifty-minute discussion, the ideal group size is four people, plus or minus one person.

These suggestions help students find groups that are more likely to be fair to all involved and rewarding to each individual. They also start students thinking from the very beginning about their groups and the responsibilities of choice. But they are also just suggestions, not laws. Every semester, I find students consciously acting against these suggestions, often with great success. As teacher, I don't try to interfere with groups that are formed which violate these suggestions. What I do instead is to comment on the violation and remind the group that it may require more work on their part. In last fall's class, for example, one group formed with three men and one woman, and when I asked them about it they collectively joked about their likelihood of excluding Susan. Yet, by the end of the tenth week, the group described Susan as their group leader. Similarly, in another group, two of the most outspoken men in class chose to work together, even though Evan was a self-proclaimed follower of Rush Limbaugh and John was a self-proclaimed politically correct liberal. When I asked them about their choice to work together, they joked about each other's "pathetic" views, but said that they respected each other and felt the opposing viewpoints would give them responses they needed. As the semester proceeded, it became clear that each man valued his opponent as a responder he could count on to be critical, and, since the other three group members gave each person supportive responses, each appreciated this criticism. In both cases, what was crucial is that these people chose their groups consciously and with some foreknowledge of the kinds of problems that might emerge. With such conscious foreknowledge, they prepared themselves for what would happen and were able to create ways for those potential problems to be beneficial to them.

What students gain by choosing their own groups is a feeling of responsibility for their group and some consciousness of the choices and potential problems that go into forming a writer's support group. When I've been able in the first few weeks of class to give students enough exposure to each other and a private opportunity to choose their group members, I've found they make sensible and productive choices for semester-long groups.

2. Developing Discussion Strategies

Along with the choice of who will be in the groups, I try to give students help making choices about the kinds of discussion they have about their writing. As with the advice I give for choosing groups, I try

to inform students at the outset of what I believe are good guiding principles for interaction, but I then let them decide what they do and help
them deal with the choices they've made.

In the very first week of class, I tell students that I want the author
of each writing to be in charge of the discussion of her piece. They, as
authors, need to develop strategies to guide discussions so that they
can get the responses they need to keep themselves writing. Consequently, I suggest that, in general, groups should divide their time
equally among the writers (for four writers, a fifty-minute period di-
vides into about twelve minutes apiece, leaving a few minutes for shuffling papers, moving chairs, and the like), and that during this time
each writer should (1) tell the responders what sort of response she
wants; (2) read the piece (or a portion of the piece) aloud; and (3) repeat
the request for response, asking direct questions where necessary.
These procedures, in general, help all of the group members feel like
they get equal treatment and can control the response they get.

I also suggest that just dividing the time equally between writers and
letting the author guide discussion isn't enough. As authors, each of us
also needs to figure out what kinds of response will (1) make us feel like
continuing to write, and (2) make us able to improve our pieces. I suggest that we need to develop strategies for response that address both
our feelings as writers and our particular writings, and that these two
needs sometimes come into conflict. Our emotional needs as writers
often include respect, support, and companionship, while our particular writing's needs often include advice for changing the content, help
imagining the needs of the best audiences for our pieces, and error
identification. The emotional needs for support and the developmental
needs for constructive criticism often are at odds, and we need to prepare for that if we are to develop effective strategies for soliciting response.

To support this point about conflicting needs, I'll often mention
Ernest Bormann's (1975) early research on small groups in the work-
place, which divided group interaction into two areas: task and maintenance. Bormann's idea was that, to function effectively, each group
not only needs to do a lot of work accomplishing the task they've set
for themselves, but also needs to do a lot of work maintaining the involvement of all group members. Bormann's research led over time to
the identification of two different leaders in most groups: a task leader
that pushed the group to get the task accomplished, and a social leader
that made sure that everyone felt good about herself or her involvement in the group. Because of the presence of these two conflicting
needs in any group, Bormann found groups in the business setting con-

sistently switching between on-task talk (such as listing ideas for how to build a better generator) and social maintenance talk (such as talk about what they did over the weekend, or about office gossip), as the groups worked to meet both their task and maintenance needs. I point out to students that, as writers, we will have both task needs (for the improvement of our writing) and maintenance needs (for continuing our motivation to write), and that we should plan to ask for response which meets both needs.

On the first Thursday of the semester, I try to model how these needs influence response by bringing in and distributing a piece of my own writing, reading it aloud to the class, and leading them through a model response session. I try in that response session to use a progression of questions that addresses both maintenance and task issues. I'll often distribute along with my writing a handout which describes a loose sequence for response which begins more on the maintenance end and moves progressively to the task end (see figures 1, 2, and 3 for examples). In class that first Thursday, I model these response strategies by having us work through them on one of my own writings. Usually, because of time constraints, I'll bring in something short like a poem or a memorandum so that it won't take much time to read the piece aloud. I do, though, try to bring in something with some emotional complexity so that students can experience, at least vicariously, some of what may be at issue in the upcoming response groups. I then ask them, as a class, to be my small group as we discuss this piece. I start with the first set of questions (figure 1), pointing out that I start with these because I'm a little nervous myself about sharing my work with people I don't yet know very well, and these strategies help me over that nervousness. After they've given some responses to the first questions, I'll stop and summarize for them what I've learned about my piece as writer and what I might try to do next. Then I'll say something like "Okay, now imagine we're three weeks further into the course, I'm feeling a lot more confident about sharing my work with you, and I'm ready for some more descriptive response." Then we'll go through the second set of strategies (figure 2), and again I'll summarize what I've learned as writer. Finally, I'll encourage us to pretend that we are even later in the course, I'm a hardened group member ready for anything, and that I want some direct revision work. We'll then do the last set of response strategies (figure 3), and I'll again summarize what I've learned as a writer about my piece. At the end of this modeling session, I'll repeat that I believe we have both maintenance and task needs as writers and need to work out strategies that will meet both needs, but that what I've offered them are suggestions, not requirements, for their own group interaction. After answering any questions, I then have class break into their first group meeting and guide the discussion of the writings they've brought in. I join whatever group seems to be having the most trouble getting going and sit in with them for the time remaining.

This first Thursday class period is always fairly intense. The initial modeling session often takes forty minutes, leaving only a half hour for their first group, and not all groups finish in that time. I also usually leave the classroom feeling very drained, probably because of the combination of self-disclosure from my writing and stress from articulating the whole range of response strategies (which give me much more response than I'm comfortable with on the piece I've brought in). But I believe that the session is worthwhile, anyway—it sets up, ahead of time, a way of responding that can guide groups effectively, and gives students time to think about response before a full attempt on their own.

Of course, by the following Thursday, when the class meets in small groups again, I find that my suggestions are only that—suggestions. I usually spend each Thursday as a participant with one small group (I bring my own writing, often a revision of what I read the week before), and invariably I find that what students actually do in groups varies considerably from what I'd suggested. Some groups start out not talking about the writing at all, but about how they wrote their pieces or how strange it feels to be writing in such a context, and the group may or may not get to all the writing. In other groups, an individual writer may ask right away for direct revision suggestions, saying he's tough and can take it, and the group may or may not feel uncomfortable giving him what he wants. In still other groups, writers may not have any questions to guide group response, saying they aren't sure what they want to know, and group members may either offer responses anyway or move to discussion of a related topic or lapse into uncomfortable silence. I can't predict how a given group will respond in the second week, even with the lengthy modeling session we've done the week before. As individuals, students need some time to experiment with response behaviors, to try out how it feels to be in groups which act these various ways, in order to decide how they will want to behave in groups as the semester progresses. Part of this experimentation, it seems to me, involves the attempt to act in writing groups as they act in other groups of their peers; part of this experimentation also involves the attempt to use or reject the strategies I suggested the week before. Such experimentation is healthy: it leads in time to the identification of strategies that do work for them as individuals, and to the identifica-

---

Initial Response Strategies
(for maintaining your motivation to write
while indirectly learning what to improve in your text)

1. Ask for *relating* responses: have your group members had an experience like the one you've had, or thoughts like those you've had? Ask them to tell you the stories of those experiences or thoughts.

2. Ask for *listening* responses: have your group tell you what they think you were saying in the piece, and where in their own experience your message would be important.

3. Ask for *positive* response: have your group point out the parts of the piece they liked best, and if possible say why.

These three kinds of response make us feel like others are listening to what we have to say, that our ideas connect with others, and that we do things well. They help us feel capable and supported as writers, and hence are very important early in our work with writing groups to develop good group maintenance. They also indirectly help us with the task of improving our pieces. The stories others tell us may spark ideas to add to our pieces; the listening responses can help us refine what exactly we are trying to say (since what they hear us saying may be slightly different from what we thought we were saying); and the sections they really liked may be ones we want to expand.

Figure 1. Initial response strategies.

tion of other people with whom they've enjoyed discussing writing. In my classes, this experimentation also leads directly to the formation of the semester-long groups they chose in week four and the patterns of interaction these long-term groups develop.

Monitoring Interaction

Because I want my students to be making informed choices about their writing, their groups, and the response they get, I require that they write out their own responses to their groups after each session. Such writing gives them a private place to reflect on what's happened in the group and how that effects their writing. This reflection is absolutely crucial. Without it, all the modeling and suggestions I offer rarely lead to conscious choices on their part. So from the very first week of class, I ask them to write reflections on their group. I support this process of reflection through class discussion, through sharing excerpts from my teaching journal with the groups, and through asking for reflection on the groups as part of their portfolio letters to me.

Second Stage Response Strategies
(for continuing to feel motivated while
working more directly on problem spots in your text)

1. Spend the first few minutes of your time continuing *relating, listening, and positive* response to assure yourself that your work is important.

2. As author, *point out the part of the text you had the most trouble writing* (it may be an idea more than a particular passage) and ask them to *describe how they reacted to it*. What did they feel/think at that point?

3. Ask each group member to give a *movie of the mind* response, describing section by section what he or she felt, thought, and imagined while reading the piece.

The two new strategies in this section both ask for descriptive responses: given that your group members have different minds than you have, you are asking them to describe how their minds make sense of what you are presenting. The "problem spot" response focuses their attention on something that bothers you as writer, and you learn how they understood that section. Maybe it didn't bother them at all; maybe they had to work to fit it into their version of your meaning; maybe they also felt it was problematic. Whatever their response, you have some information with which to consider changes in the piece. The "movie of the mind" response is like the "problem spot" response, only for the piece as a whole. Be forewarned: a good "movie of the mind" response will tell you a lot about your text and highlight portions of it that are working very differently than you imagine!

Figure 2. Second stage response strategies.

To help establish the habit of such reflection, I build reflection into the Thursday sessions during the first five weeks of class. On Thursdays before they meet in groups, I ask the students to write privately on their own for two to three minutes about what they want to know from their group today. After the groups meet, I leave about fifteen minutes of class time at the end of each Thursday class period to use for reflection. I have the groups stop discussing and invite the students to write privately for five minutes about the group and their writing, addressing in any order they wish Elbow and Belanoff's three process log questions: "What happened?" "What do I think of my writing now?" and "What will I do next?" After we've written, I read my reflection aloud, asking for a couple of volunteers to read theirs aloud, too, and then I ask for comments or questions. This open sharing of reflections helps establish the habit of reflecting after group meetings and also helps everyone in class see some of the range of reactions people have to their group discussions.

Direct-Task Response Strategies
(for use when you're confident about the piece,
and yourself as writer, and want to improve the piece)

1. Spend some of your time doing *relating, listening, and positive* response to assure yourself of your idea's importance and your ability.

2. Ask group members to point out *parts they didn't like or had trouble with* and have them explain why.

3. Ask them, if it were their piece, *what changes they would make* and why.

These response strategies go right for the challenging parts of improving a piece—identifying what might be changed and exploring options for change. If you use these strategies, remember that it's your piece, even though you are asking group members to respond as if the piece was their own. You may want to consider the suggestions they make carefully, but in the end it's your piece and you decide whether or not to take their advice. (You'll probably also find that different people give different advice for change, if you ask them.)

Figure 3. Direct-task response strategies.

Here are the process logs Deb wrote about her group meetings in weeks two, three, and four of my fall 1992 class (in week one, we didn't do a process log in class because we ran out of time):

Week Two Process Log

I really like the group we had today. Everyone has a different perspective on our writings and has a similar (or can find a similar) situation to talk about. We *like* to *talk!* We didn't get a chance to talk much about the last three writings because we became so involved in what was written before. I felt comfortable reading my paper to these people, and wish we had more time to share our feelings. I know I want to expand my paper in more detail. There is more I can compare in my life that will work in with this paper. Each time I read this I can see something new and the group also helped me devise some new thoughts. I need to expand on the flying aspect for the bird and for life.

Week Three Process Log

[Before group]: I went to a leadership conference last weekend that dealt with attitudes a lot. It really opened up my mind and how you can control many unnecessary feelings. I hope people will *agree* with my paper (message) but question it. I hope we talk about both sides, but can come to terms with these opinions.

[After group]: After talking to my group, we were really concerned with all of our attitudes (in school especially). We decided

we all take many things for granted. We believe there is no need to
be fake about "Having a bad day" because we all do. We just need
to watch these attitudes we oversee.

We also talked about how to go about writing about my brother
and my relationship because it is something I want to do, but I'm
not sure how to go about it. I am the oldest and the others in my
group are the youngest and speaking with them I now have a new
idea of what to try. I might even try to speak from my brother's
point of view.

Week Four Process Log

[Before group] I rewrote one of my first papers using the techniques we had discussed earlier. I really got a lot more out of it this
time, especially since I hadn't looked at it for over a month. I hope
the response I get out of it is enjoyment. I wrote it for myself, but
think it turned into something that can be universal.

[After group] The use of the revision technique really helped my
paper. I think everyone had heard my first draft and I enjoyed how
they enjoyed the new aspects I had added to it.

I am leaving class more excited to write about two new topics
I've never thought about writing. I kept having to stop our conversation so I could write these ideas down. I think our group really works well together and I am looking forward to next
Tuesday's class reading to learn and get ideas from everyone else.

Deb's process logs provide a glimpse of what happened in her groups
(both the random groups of the first four weeks and her continuing
group after that point) and how the groups altered what happened. For
example, it's clear from her first process log that her group spent all
their time on just two students' writing, one of which was hers, and that
she's aware this is a problem ("we didn't get a chance to talk about the
last three writings"). By week three, this comment has disappeared; by
week four, she mentions how many "new ideas" she is getting from listening to her group's pieces and hence how much she's looking forward to the full-class reading of finished work in week five. This
progression suggests that by week four, Deb's group has found a way
to share time more equitably so that she is excited about what all her
group members are writing, not just what she writes.

But Deb's process logs also show her gradually gaining perspective
on her own work through the group sessions. In her week two process
log, she writes only that she wants to provide more detail in her piece
and that the group provided some new thoughts, but she seems unable
at this point to give herself many concrete suggestions or to imagine
what to do with her group's response. This changes dramatically in her
week three process log, where she writes directly about the difference
in perspective she has as the oldest child in her family and those of her

group members as the youngest children in their families, and she speculates about writing from the point of view of her brother. I get the sense from this process log that much of the talk about her piece in week three was relating talk (the group told stories of their own attitude adjustment problems and about how they, as youngest children, perceive their older siblings), and that this talk was much more important to Deb than the vague brainstorming of new ideas in the week before. Her process log suggests that she felt supported by the group's connection to her attitude piece and found herself challenged by the difference in perspective between youngest and oldest siblings. The result of this support and challenge is a new idea for her writing—a conscious attempt to take on the perspective of someone other than herself. This idea seems to be something she assigned herself at the end of the group meeting; there's nothing to suggest that a group member directly advised her to try it. By the fourth week, Deb's awareness of what she might try in her writing has continued, and she seems to be expecting to be prompted into new thoughts just by hearing the different things her group writes and says. She writes of being pleased with her attempts to revise her first piece and with group response—but what's most on her mind are the ideas for new pieces she's come up with just by listening to others read.

By taking part in her group and then reflecting on it afterward, Deb is gradually becoming aware of the way she uses her group's responses to find ideas and to see where she can revise her pieces. In her portfolio letter at week five, it was these aspects of group interaction that she focused on:

> My small group has helped me see other perceptions than my own. They will find a sentence or a phrase that will spark something from their own memory. Through this I can get new ideas and add them to my own. . . . At first my group intimidated me because they never questioned my work. I am always looking for a new way to try things and don't believe they could possibly understand everything I wrote down. After putting a piece of work away for a while, and coming back to it a week later, even I don't understand it. Recently, we have been working more collectively together because I have learned to ask specific questions about what I have written. Sometimes I think we know each other so well they understand me more than what is written. I feel very comfortable talking to my group members. We are alike in many ways, but have totally different backgrounds. I have been "stealing" from their minds without them knowing. HA HA! That's the best part of being in a small group. . . . I hope that we could get copies and send copies home with each other of some of our final work. I think it would be interesting not to talk about it, but read it ourselves and

write comments on the bottom. Comments of what they liked,
what they didn't, what they would change, and what they could
relate to. I think then we could really get some unbiased opinions
and people could truly express how they feel without any pressure.

Deb lists here some of the same features of group interaction that she
mentioned in her weekly logs: the importance of the new perspective
they offer, the fact that she steals ideas from them without them knowing, and her worry about not getting detailed enough responses to her
work. She also describes the group as working better together as time
has passed (the groups have become permanent, and she is guiding her
group's responses with her own questions). And lastly, she is aware of
what the group isn't offering her yet and spends some time devising
strategies for getting what she needs: the group, she hints, is too nice to
her writing even though she knows there are flaws in it, so she suggests
some written feedback as a way to get more "unbiased" response to her
work.

If you compare what Deb says about her group with what she wrote
about her own writing process (presented above in the portfolio section
of this chapter), you'll see that Deb's experience with her group has led
her to an awareness of her need to understand revision. Where she
began class believing she could write with little effort the kind of analogies that Robert Fulghum writes, by week five she's aware that she usually doesn't start out understanding what's most important about an
experience and that she needs strategies to help her rework her pieces
to capture what's most important. What she writes about her small
group suggests that their responses have been instrumental in her
reaching these conclusions. Although she doesn't say so directly, it
sounds as though she has been surprised repeatedly by the perspectives they offer on her ideas, and these perspectives have prompted her
to think that there's more to her topics than she had first imagined.
Coupled with the challenge of these fresh perspectives, though, is a
sense of the group's relative inability to show her how to rework her
pieces, quite possibly because they don't see the shock of their perspectives the same way she does. Deb writes that "I think we know
each other so well they understand me more than what is written," suggesting that in group discussion, her group members think they are
summarizing her writing for her in ways that capture what she's said,
while she finds their summaries bringing in new ideas that she didn't
know were there. Deb is aware of the gaps between their summaries
and her intentions and wants to develop strategies to revise using the
awareness of her content these responses provide her. Her group members, on the other hand, may only be aware of their support of her ideas

and may not see these gaps. Thus, by the point of week five, Deb is ready both socially and individually to focus her attention on revision strategies that allow for more honest description of what is actually in her texts and what is only in her thinking about the texts, as well as for ways to make her texts reflect more of the richness of her thinking.

Thus, Deb's growth as a writer in these five weeks occurs in response to her small group's interaction. She finds herself more and more aware of a personal need to understand revision because her group discussions have convinced her that she doesn't fully understand her ideas when she first sits down to write: the group discussion always provides her with new material she wants to address. But she doesn't reach this conclusion about herself because someone in the group articulates it for her. In fact, at this point her group members may be unaware that she feels a gap between her writing and their perspectives. It's in the response to her group that Deb's learning occurs, not necessarily in the group discussion itself. And that's why the process logs, portfolio letters, and goal-setting sessions are so important: they provide the students with opportunities to set down their responses to their group sessions in order to see how their responses need to guide their future writing.

Of course, not all students are able to find a productive use of groups as quickly as Deb did. Many students, in fact, find themselves with one of two less-productive responses to their groups: either they enjoy the group interaction but aren't sure how that interaction connects with their writing, or they find themselves frightened of the group interaction and fear the group's evaluation of them through their writing. For such students, just providing the reflection opportunities of process logs and portfolio letters may not be enough. With such students, I find myself using my teaching journal and my own interactions in their groups to help them see ways of monitoring their own responses to groups.

Doug's group experience is a good example of the need for these extra ways to prompt reflection. Doug was a pre-med junior when he took my course. In his goal conferences with me, he expressed interest in writing (especially the sort of personal writing about professional lives that Richard Seltzer, Lewis Thomas, and Stephen Jay Gould do), but his first few process logs seemed vague and uninformative:

Week Two Process Log

As always in groups, we started off as unfamiliar people, but, through our writings, and discussion of common experiences and parts of our lives, we made contact. The group experience was good, and we decided to stick together for the time being. As far as my work is concerned, I will stick with a portion and then expand it.

Week Four Process Log

I do like my group—we kind of hit it off, I think. Today, I read the short paper entitled "Travelogue," and then just talked about how close that place is to me. This paper really came out without much hard work—I guess it "flowed." I'll probably continue to rewrite this work for reading by others. Once again Abigail encouraged me about my paper, and told me I had good ideas—so I had to thank her.

Doug's process logs described good feelings about his group work, but also a kind of vagueness about where those good feelings came from or how they impacted his writing. He claimed to like his group, enjoying the sharing of life stories and Abigail's supportive comments, but he also seemed mystified about where his pieces came from or how the group affected them ("This paper really came out without much hard work—I guess it 'flowed'."). Unlike Deb, he seemed unable to articulate how or if the group experience connected with his writing.

Now the group context in which Doug wrote may have had something to do with this. Where Deb formed a group at week four that included two people she'd worked with from the start of the semester, Doug purposefully worked in a different group each of the three experimental weeks (when he made his lists of preferred group members on Tuesday of the fourth week, I learned that he'd been trying to get out of groups with a former girlfriend, which is why he didn't stay in the first group he was in). After week four, when permanent groups were created, Doug's group members had a rush of attendance problems. One student dropped the course after evaluations in week six. The other two group members, Abigail and June, each caught the midwestern flu and were gone for two Thursday meetings (not the same days) between week four and week eight. As a consequence, Doug did not experience the consistency in group interaction that Deb experienced, and this inconsistency in group experience may have contributed to his general sense of vagueness about how the group affected his writing.

Since I was aware of the troubles in Doug's group, I chose to participate in his group two weeks in a row near the middle of the semester. In general, I try to become a participant in the groups that seem most in need of help on any given Thursday. I choose which groups to work with from some combination of body language (a group that won't form a circle, for example, and instead stays spread out in a loose line often is showing unwillingness or uncertainty about working together), attendance problems (a group where two people are absent is hardly large enough for a group), or direct requests for help (students will often ask for help in the writing they submit to me every two weeks). I worked with Doug's group one week when all three group members were there, and then the following week when only June and Doug attended. Since Doug and his group members seemed to be enjoying working together but were having trouble (Doug especially) connecting their writing and their group experience, I used my presence to model some ways of reflecting on writing groups.

The most important modeling was the sharing of a section from my teaching journal. Once a week in a teaching journal, I try to write out my reflections of what's happening in my writing classes, primarily for my own thinking. I often find, though, that this writing is something I can bring to share as my contribution with groups on Thursdays—especially when I can tie these reflections to beginning thoughts toward some professional article I am writing. After I met with Doug's group, I tried in my teaching journal to describe what had happened during the group session, and the following week I distributed those reflections during my writing time. (Since I was writing this book at the time, I tied my investigation of their group to the fact that I was already writing about writing groups.) Here's what I shared with them:

> This week, I worked with June, Abigail, and Doug. They all stared at me to start with and joked about going first, and June asked me to go first, so I did, with my piece (the start of a book on small groups). I asked for help with tone, or at least a description of what they thought of tone. Doug and June both gave useful descriptions here—Doug with a caveat about feeling he was responding to me as I appear in class more than me as I appear in the writing. June said she thought I was "laid back" and "down to earth" and pointed to places in the text where she thought I showed these things. Doug read after me, a piece about his dad—then he talked about his dad and his memories for about eight minutes. No real response, except nonverbal support, from us, but Doug concludes by saying he feels we've helped and he knows where to go next. Apparently, he talked his way through a problem. Abigail then read a piece about spouse abuse, general at first and then tied to her own marriage. She followed this with a statement that she really has good stuff in her life, too, and will write about it sometime, but first she wants to get out this stuff that seems to come when she sits down to write. June says how much she learns from Abigail's writing because she hasn't experienced it herself but has friends she's trying to understand, who do. Doug nods. We spend time talking mainly about why these topics are important to write about, sort of setting a context of importance around her risky work—as I think back on it, a lot of this group's conversation fol-

lows this pattern: talk not directly about the text; talk instead about placing the idea in context, making it important personally to each other first, and to the writing, and comparing it to needs people have. They also talked some about themselves as a group—they perceive themselves as a "good group" because they are support- ive and honest, and I think they are right. They are each writing re- flectively on fairly major, challenging personal subjects, allowing themselves to act as writers, and using the group more for *support* as they try out that writing tempo than for *response* to the pieces di- rectly. Thus Doug brings in journal pages about his dad and talks through the memories of his thinking; Abigail brings in writing about her struggles with abuse and talks through the importance of addressing these issues. . . .

After reading this piece aloud during my group time, I asked for their sense of the accuracy of this description. I explained that I was considering using this piece as an example in my writing on groups and wanted to test if I'd got the description right. In group, June and Doug then spent a few minutes each offering their versions of their small groups. They both agreed that they valued the topics they were sharing, that they wanted to support each other, and that they both felt they were ready for some more direct feedback on the writings as well as the supportive talk about the importance of their subjects. And, that day, group went on much as it had the week before.

Functionally, the group members used my piece as a chance to talk about their group interaction. First, they affirmed that they valued the group the way it was—they enjoyed each other's work and the support they received. But second, they identified feelings they both had of wanting a bit more directed response to their writings, and by an- nouncing these desires, they allowed themselves to change the direc- tion of their group interaction a bit.

The following week I received a paper and a process log from Doug which showed that he and June were experimenting with new ways of responding:

> I have been doing my journals, but they have been kind of half- assed, so for a change of pace last week I sat down to write a piece more for a reader. So I began a piece about my summer vacation spot. . . . In my group today (with June) we traced the processes in- volved in my new paper about "the lake." I have written on the draft you'll get where we think the piece was going in different sec- tions. There is such a volume of material I could produce about this place, and that came evident to me by seeing how many different ideas I incorporated into this paper. I may try to "transpose" the first two paragraphs into poetry because June suggested it may work. In your reading of my paper, do you see the same divisions of ideas that June and I did?

Apparently, Doug and June spent the following week's group focused very narrowly on the text itself, with the result that Doug tried his first-ever poem for the next Tuesday's class. Doug found the close analysis of his writing beneficial to him, and in the weeks that followed began doing his own close responses to his writings in process logs after he wrote. His group continued to spend most of their time supporting each other's topic with a bit of textual analysis thrown in, but he now had some ways of responding privately to his writing that enhanced his group discussions. In other words, Doug gradually created a way of using both process logs and group discussion to provide support for and analysis of his writing. Where he began class feeling good about groups but not being sure how they connected to his writing, he left class with a strong sense of the link between process logs and group support—a link he made explicitly in his final portfolio letter:

> The next section to be discussed is the one that I never thought I would actually love as much as I did this semester. In previous classes, group work involved saying "I liked it," "It is well-written," or "I agree with your ideas," while smiling and nodding and inside sometimes feeling totally opposite, but not wanting to say so. This could be partly my own fault, but it just seemed like the way to act in a group setting. Then I got matched up in this class with two women with great ideas, important problems to be dealt with, and wonderful friendship to be shared. . . . The input I received from my group-mates was beneficial to my semester. Whether it be a simple nod or smile, or a spoken or written way in which to get my point across better, I appreciated and used almost every ounce of suggestion and encouragement. . . . I feel that I learned how to better respond to myself once I have something down on paper. The process log is key to this method. I would write down a sentence or two after an essay or journal, basically deciding where I wished to go with it. To continue or not to continue. To add or subtract from it. To change it into poetry. . . . In my groups, as I mentioned above, I learned a lot about what I had written and where it sounded like it was going. But another facet that I didn't realize until you read a portion of your teaching journal to my group was that I would often talk my own way through a quandary. The nods of my fellow group members encouraged me to continue talking, until I had made a decision about my own writing. . . . I still thank my group for this, because otherwise the forum would never have been there for me to speak my mind and synthesize ideas like I could with my group, who understood where I was, where I wanted to be, and how I felt.

Doug connects his talking through a problem with his group's support to the private decision making of process logs, and he sees the two as all mixed together in the general experience of response to his writing.

In short, Doug developed effective ways of connecting the group experience and his own writing process, once he received some personalized modeling that pointed him and his group in the direction of those connections. Where students like Deb seem to be able to make such connections on their own when they find themselves in a supportive, analytic small group, students like Doug may need our help to design their own interventions in their small-group experience—especially when, as in Doug's group, the group experience begins inconsistently.

My job as teacher, thus, is to establish patterns for monitoring small-group interaction which can help students like Deb and Doug. Setting up regular reflection times is enough to prompt many students, like Deb, to articulate their own uses of small-group response. For other students, like Doug, my job as teacher may be to model particular kinds of reflection which can help them overcome the blocks they experience in group interaction, knowing of course that they will make unique, individual uses of whatever modeling I do.

Experiencing Diversity

While response and reflection are the most important and immediate functions of small groups in writing workshops, a third function is to provide exposure to diversity. For students to make informed choices about the future place of writing in their lives, they need to be exposed to a range of uses of writing, to the many ways people use writing to interact with their worlds. With such exposure, students can begin to choose the uses of writing that seem most important to them. With opportunities to explore these choices once they see some of the range that's available, students can leave a writing workshop with experiences that can inform their later uses of writing.

In small groups of the sort I've described, students invariably experience a range of writing just by attending and reading each other's pieces. In most groups, the diversity of writing that students attempt when they are allowed to make their own topic and genre choices is stunning. It clearly demonstrates that we, as teachers, don't need to feel responsible for bringing diversity into our classrooms (through assigned multicultural readers, for example), because diversity already exists amid the people we teach. Even in Nebraska classrooms, where students by and large come from a single geographic area and by and large share many ethnic, religious, and cultural traits, the amount of diversity that exists is encouraging.

Let me give examples of what I mean by such diversity by describing the writing of two groups in my fall 1992 class. Both groups, to the eye, seemed homogeneous: one group had three women and one man, the other three men and one woman; all group members were white, mid-twenties, middle-class students who grew up in the state of Nebraska. But when we survey the writing each group did, it's clear that even in their seeming homogeneity the groups were quite diverse.

In the first group, the four people wrote widely different things. Elizabeth spent most of her semester working on a proposal for a senior thesis on Alzheimer's treatment, bringing in writing that struggled with the standard American Psychological Association organization for psychology journals. But she also wrote several drafts of an essay on stereotyping, using as her examples the clash on campus between fraternities and sororities on the one hand and independents on the other. Jocelyn, by contrast, wrote mainly personal journals and poetry. Her journals addressed her bouts with depression, her feelings about her husband's return to the Persian Gulf as part of the ongoing Air Force peacekeeping effort, and her frustrations with school. Her poetry was blatantly imagistic—the one poem she worked on most described a caged lioness. Midway through the semester, her grandmother died, and after a two-week absence Jocelyn began collecting and retelling family memories of her grandmother in a sort of chapbook for her relatives. Keith, the only male member of the group, spent the first part of the semester writing what he called "idea pieces" about the nature of Mind, based on discussions from his philosophy class that intrigued him. But about eight weeks into the semester, he began bringing in widely different pieces each week—a description of one of his favorite video games, a meditation on the changes he'd lived through on his father's ranch in the sandhills of western Nebraska, a journal about a friend's child custody battle for which he was a character witness in court. Val, the last member of this group, was a member of Queer Nation, the gay and lesbian rights group. She spent the bulk of her semester writing a variety of lesbian-issue pieces: an analysis of how her own coming out had influenced her family; a long poem describing male and female gazes toward women; an essay on drag. Val, however, also wrote two pieces that had nothing to do with this dominant theme: a nostalgic look at her childhood imagination and a descriptive nature piece on the coming of fall.

Once I list the range of writing that occurred in this group, my initial perception of homogeneity disappears and what emerges instead is a sense of the range of experience and writing the group members offer each other. Elizabeth and Keith use writing to explore ideas and academic thinking; Joyce and Val bring in attempts at aesthetic, imagistic poetry; Val, Elizabeth, and Keith use their writing to confront major social issues, from both personal and political standpoints; at different times, Joyce, Val, and Keith all use writing to explore personal feelings or traumas through the semiprivate vehicle of an unrevised journal. As the semester continued, the other group members exposed each individual to a range of issues for writing and a range of uses of writing that they had not considered initially. Often, this exposure led to those same individuals trying out some of these other uses of writing—often in contrast to their initial week two goals. Keith, for example, began the course saying he never liked the personal writing he'd had to do in first-year composition and preferred writing about ideas—he and I shared an admiration for writers like Stephen Jay Gould and Carl Sagan who explain ideas clearly for educated lay people. But by midway through the semester, Keith was trying his hand at exactly the personal writings he had rejected earlier, using a journal to sort through his courtroom experience and a personal essay to address the changes on his family's ranch. Clearly, his vicarious exposure to the personal writing that Jocelyn and Val were doing proved attractive to him, allowing him to explore a use of writing he had previously rejected.

The diversity of writing in this small group is the norm rather than the exception, I've found. Almost all groups end up showing something of the same diversity. In the other representative group from my fall 1992 class, a similar range of diversity appears (with perhaps the exception of a writer as openly courageous as Val about confronting a potentially hostile community). In the second group, Susan wrote an essay bemoaning the anti-intellectualism she sees among students and faculty on campus, a story/essay comparing African initiation rites she'd studied in anthropology class to the twenty-first birthday ritual she sees around her on campus, a poem, and a long piece filled with childhood memories and descriptions about the values she feels she learned from her mother. By contrast, Brad initially wrote a series of one-page descriptions of such things as what he sees while lying on his couch, but then switched to writing two longer pieces, one describing a conversation he had with a childhood sweetheart which basically addressed the differences they'd developed since leaving the small western Nebraska town in which they'd grown up, the other presenting a day from his life as an Army private stationed in Germany, in which he tried to describe the boredom, substance abuse, and prejudice that he experienced. Chuck wrote poetry, a story depicting graduation from high school as "the first death" a person experiences in life, a number of humorous pieces modeled on Dave Barry's columns, and several uncompleted short stories. Dennis, the last member of this group, wrote two articles about the Nebraska football team and a eulogy to his father before he dropped out of class in week six.

As in the first group, the work of Susan, Brad, Chuck, and Dennis exposed each other to a wide variety of uses and purposes for writing. Chuck showed what could be done with humor. Susan and Chuck brought in persuasive essays of the sort printed in editorials. Susan and Brad brought in highly complex stories/essays addressing personal and social issues. And, as in the first group, the existence of this range of pieces created opportunities for individuals to try out uses of writing they hadn't previously imagined. Brad changed dramatically from writing the sort of descriptive pieces he told me he associated with English classes to complex essay/stories of the sort Susan was writing. Susan tried her hand at poetry and humor, largely because Chuck's work made it seem possible. As in the first group, the exposure each person received to a wider range of writing increased the kinds of writing each felt willing to attempt. For developing writers, such exposure is one of the most positive and growthful aspects of the small-group experience. Individuals find their range of writing increasing almost magically because they see weekly what other real people do with writing and why it is beneficial to them. As Deb put it, one of the best things about small groups is that you get to steal from each other.

Of course, the positive aspects of this exposure are accompanied by risks—risks that the diversity will be too great, individuals will feel too challenged or too uncertain about themselves, and will close down their writing. Every semester, my teaching journal fills up with instances where I confront these risks, worrying about students who will find the class's diversity a barrier rather than an invitation to writing. About ten weeks into the class, for example, I wrote:

> Last Thursday, due to several absences, two groups combined partial members to form a one-day response group. Arnold and Shannon from one group; Elizabeth and Val from another. As I watched this group form in class, I expected fireworks: Arnold is continuing his "call to the ministry" piece; Val has been writing lesbian role poetry; Shannon has been writing about being black in Nebraska; and Elizabeth has been writing a psychology proposal. The class period before, Arnold had sneered at a woman who had exchanged angry editorials about animal rights with him in the *Daily Nebraskan*, and Val had defended this woman—and I suspected this was the exchange that caused Val to speak to me privately of her feelings that the environment was hostile toward her. I figured I *had* to get into this group, both because they might need some help mitigating strife, and because it would be interesting. (I'd talked to both Arnold and Val outside of class last week because both had felt silenced on Tuesday, both feeling like their positions had been too far from the norm and were misheard—interesting since the two are on polar opposite ends of the political spectrum: a devout Christian and an out lesbian. And *both* felt silenced.)

The negative side of diversity is silence—the silence of withdrawal because you feel that the others aren't listening to what you have to say or are making negative judgments about you; the silence of oppression because you feel the expression of your opinions might put you at some kind of risk. As intriguing and interesting as diversity is—because each of us gets exposed to ways of thought and action that are wonderfully different from our own, and we thus get curious—it can also be experienced as threatening—because we do in fact teach in a world where people sometimes suffer physical or verbal abuse for their opinions and self-expressions.

In dealing with this risky side of diversity, I am guided by the same principles that guide my use of small groups in general: the individual learner, and not me as teacher, should be the one to decide what stance to take toward the diversity that exists. Just as I ask students to decide what groups they will work in after experimentation and guided reflection, just as I ask students to decide how to use the response they get to their pieces after experimentation and guided reflection, I believe students need to make their own decisions about their response to such diversity after experimentation and guided reflection.

I don't think I have any right as teacher to push students to write publicly about subjects they are not comfortable sharing—they should decide what stays private in their writing and what they bring to group. Similarly, I don't feel I have a right to restrict students from writing pieces that are really important to them—Arnold and Val both have good reasons for exploring their controversial subjects publicly. What I feel I must do, though, is provide opportunities in my classroom for the range of diversity that exists to be visible in the classroom, and I must also provide opportunities for each individual to reflect on what this diversity means for him or her and on how the student personally wants to respond to it.

In practice, this stance toward diversity has meant that I schedule into class a number of forums for the public expression of one's views and surround these forums with reflective writing opportunities.

Obviously, the small groups themselves are one such forum. Each week, students share material with each other, share responses to that material, and then write their own reflections about the interactions in their process logs. In any given group any given week, individuals will thus already be dealing with the positive and negative sides of exposure. The other students in Arnold's and Val's groups, for example, had to decide fairly early on how they would react to these people's writings. It didn't surprise me, consequently, to learn on the fourth Tuesday of class that both Arnold and Val appeared more frequently than other students on the class's wish lists for group members. Many students had their curiosity tweeked by Arnold's and Val's writing and hence wanted to be in groups with one of them, but Arnold's and Val's names also showed up on a fair number of "don't put me in a group with so-and-so" lists. Students were clearly making up their own minds about how much diversity they could handle in groups.

But I also try to provide several other forums for public sharing and private reflection, all of which serve to surround each student's writing with continued exposure to the variety of writing that exists in class. Of these, the most important are the class public readings of our best work, which take place during weeks five and ten and at finals week, when the students submit their portfolios. During these weeks, the normal Tuesday/Thursday structure for the course is suspended, and instead we take turns reading aloud the work we've completed. For a class of twenty to twenty-four students, this reading usually takes two class periods. My structure for it is fairly straightforward: we begin with a volunteer (I usually ask who needs to get it over with first) and then proceed clockwise around the classroom. After each person's reading, there is a round of what I call "loud spontaneous applause" (a term I borrowed from Les Whipp, the director of the Nebraska Writing Project during my first years at the University of Nebraska). During the last five to ten minutes of each reading period, I invite students to write short fan letters to the three or four people whose writing they most respected, and to give them these letters before class ends.

These public readings are a powerful way to let everyone in class hear the diverse range of writing that exists in each class. In preparation for these readings, individuals need to think about what they've written and what of this they are willing to read, and in doing so confront many of the silence issues about which they need to make decisions. In responding to the class readings—through writing fan letters, receiving fan letters, and reflecting about the experience in their process logs—individuals find themselves identifying uses of writing that attract them and perhaps writings that frighten them as well. Interestingly, these reading days are often commented on by students as the best days of the whole semester: in the words of one student, "I didn't care for reading myself too much, but I loved hearing everybody else read. We have some incredible writing going on."

Besides these public reading days, I also try to provide students with at least one other opportunity each semester to address the whole class publicly on a subject of their choice. In recent semesters, I've experimented with several formats for such opportunities. One year, I used "town meetings," as described by my colleague Gerry Brookes (1993):

each week, one or two students are given five to ten minutes to address the class on a subject of concern to them, to lead a short discussion on that subject, and to get some written feedback about it. Students talk about rudeness to bicyclists, about parking, student elections, athletics, endorsements of political candidates, whatever they see as important to talk about. Another year, I tried "book talks" (an idea I borrowed from Calkins's elementary school classrooms): each week, one or two students take five to ten minutes to talk about a book (or other writing) they really admire, read a section aloud, lead a short discussion, and get some written feedback. In last fall's class, book talks covered such diverse items as Terry McMillan's *Waiting to Exhale* (1992), Susan Faludi's *Backlash* (1991), Rush Limbaugh's *The Way Things Ought To Be* (1992), Ayn Rand's *Atlas Shrugged* (1957), and the children's book by John Scieszka, *The True Story of the Three Little Pigs* (1989). Another year, I tried "open letters," in which groups of individuals decide on a topic or reading they all are interested in, distribute this reading to the class along with letters each of them has written in response to it, and then guide a twenty-minute discussion and written-feedback session the following class period.

Each of these forums provides yet another way for students to acknowledge and address the diversity that exists in any class of twenty people. Individually, they hear what each other has to say, they decide what they themselves are comfortable sharing with their class, and they respond to what each person brings up. I tend to schedule whichever of these I'm using a given semester into the first ten minutes of class each day, thus providing each student at least one opportunity to address the whole class during the semester, and surrounding all students weekly with the experience of listening to what someone else thinks is important. It doesn't take much class time, and the return in exposure to new ideas is tremendous. These whole-class activities are ways to extend the exposure to new uses of writing that students receive from their small groups and to extend the individual reflection on this exposure that is crucial to the informed choices students will later make about the place of writing in their lives.

Groups and Writers' Lives

It's a common experience for me, a semester or two after having taught a writing course, to run into one of my students cashiering in the local Super Saver grocery store, or shopping for Christmas presents in Gateway Mall. One of the things these people often want to tell me is whether or not they are still writing: "I had a piece accepted in *Laurus* [the undergraduate literary magazine]," June said when I saw her this January, for example. Even when they can't remember my name (which is frequently the case), they remember some excitement about writing and want to tell me where they are now with that writing.

Interestingly, when I get to talking with these former students in such chance meetings, the single thing that most predicts whether or not they are still writing is the existence of a supportive writing group. The students who are still writing have found ways to form such groups for themselves, whether the groups are part of our undergraduate creative writing program or part of an on-the-job group like the *Daily Nebraskan* newspaper staff or an offshoot of some other support group, like the writing group that split off from Abigail's Twelve-Step Program or Arnold's Christian writing group or Judy's feminist reading group. And the students who have stopped writing often say the same thing—they haven't found anyone to share their writing with and have lost motivation trying to write by themselves.

The exposure, response, and community offered by groups clearly are the most important ingredients of a writer's life which my classes can offer my students. We all write, just as we engage in any other activity, because the behavior is valued by others whom we care about; we continue writing because the act surrounds us with social response we value. If we really want our students to benefit from a writer's life, to find ways of making writing part of the lives they lead, then we need to help them experience the kind of community in which writing grows. And we need to help them define for themselves the essential features of such communities so that they can create such groups themselves outside the artificial contexts of our classes. In my experience, immersing students in writerly behaviors and helping them develop the monitoring strategies that help them articulate what's personally essential about those behaviors is one way to invite students into the communal life of writing—a life which I believe increases the quality of lived experience, no matter what particular form it takes.

6 Changing the Frame: Writing, Reading, and Learning about Writing in Small Groups

Rick Evans
University of Nebraska–Lincoln

> I knew I could trust my audience. . . . I could write.
>
> —Excerpt from Kristi's reflective writing

At the beginning of the semester, I wrote a story/letter to one of my high school English teachers, Mr. Kolterman. He was my favorite teacher and was dying of cancer; I wanted him to know how I felt through my writing. After reading my draft . . . to my group, they wanted to know more about him; they wanted me to show how Mr. Kolterman inspired me. I followed up with a descriptive story, sharing the experience of the day that influenced me the most. As I wrote about him, my group grew more and more familiar with the emotions behind my stories and my need to write about him. Later in the semester I wrote a poem about Mr. Kolterman and his illness. There was a part of the poem that wasn't working for me, but I wasn't sure why. My group, [knowing] my feelings [for] Mr. Kolterman, helped me identity what wasn't working. . . . Without a constant, stable group throughout the semester, I don't think I would have continued writing about [a] subject . . . I so desperately needed to write about!

> —Excerpt from Deb's reflective writing

Small groups are the places to try out new ideas, make sense of old ones and help others do the same. . . . Members bring their writings and read them to the rest of the group, and then the group responds. . . . I can still remember some of the pieces that my group members brought to the group. Shannon wrote a story about [a] couple who lost a baby. Andy wrote a story about prejudice on campus. Heather wrote a piece about her mother, and Kristi [a white woman] wrote a letter to her parents explaining her relationship with her boyfriend [a black man]. . . . [The] small group serves as a real audience for the writers. [Typically] writers are motivated to write what the teacher wants instead of what the writer [herself] wants. When [she] writes for the teacher, [her] main goal is to get a good grade. However, when [she] has a real audience, the writer is motivated to reach her audience. [She] wants her writing to be understood by her small group. [She] wants the group to be able to identify/relate to what has been written.

—Excerpt from Jacque's reflective
writing

I grew a great deal from my experience. I have learned to become a better writer from the constructive criticism I received as well as from the strengths that were identified in my writing. I learned how to give constructive criticism and identify strengths also. [Previously,] I would read a piece for grammatical and punctuation errors without much exertion of energy. But, that isn't the process. It takes a lot of work, time, energy, and care to be a responder. . . . [Consequently,] I became a much better reader. . . . [My] small group experience . . . gave me the opportunity to grow. . . .

—Excerpt from Adena's reflective
writing

One of the courses that I most enjoy teaching at the University of Nebraska–Lincoln is English 457, "Composition Theory and Practice." It is a course that offers students the opportunity to write and read, to talk and listen, and to think about the teaching of writing in a workshop setting. The students themselves are juniors and seniors, all from our neighboring Teachers College, and generally interested in teaching in a middle school or high school. Most want to teach English, some social studies, and a few natural sciences and/or mathematics. An ideal group of students? In many ways, they are. They want to be teachers. Good teachers. They want to be the kind of teachers that their future students will remember, just as they themselves remember some of their former teachers. They want to make a difference in their students' lives, and they want me to tell them how. The problem, at least when the course begins, is that what I want to tell them, they are as yet unable, or better said, unready, to hear. They are unable or unready because most continue to understand classroom teaching and learning according to the "traditional conventions" outlined now more than two decades ago by Kenneth A. Bruffee (1972). For example, typically they assume that the only important classroom relationship is that "one-to-one relationship" between themselves as individual (and isolated) students and their teacher (Bruffee 1972, 459). They believe that they learn only when they talk in response to the teacher's questions or when the teacher talks at them. They believe that the only aim or purpose in writing is to demonstrate to the teacher what they have learned; and that, in turn, the teacher must evaluate their learning, indeed correct their demonstration by pointing to what they have failed to learn. Finally, these students rarely recognize genuine open-ended interaction or collaboration of any kind among themselves or with their teacher as a valid learning experience. Actually, such interaction or collaboration is "highly suspect," sometimes even "considered to be the worst possible academic sin" (Bruffee 1972, 459), the sin of "softness" (Elbow 1991b, 210). Similarly, when they imagine themselves as teachers, they often select between one of two roles: lecturer or tutor—both mirror reflections of their understanding of themselves as students. The lecturer "talks or performs, and the students watch and listen" (Bruffee 1972, 459). Conversely, the tutor watches and listens as individual students present or perform what they have learned. These are the ways of being students and teachers that they not only accept, but have been led through their years and years of successful schooling (i.e., getting good grades) to expect.

However, in my classroom, I attempt to offer them the *experience*, or better said, attempt to allow them to offer themselves the experience of different ways of being students and teachers in a school context, different ways of being and behaving as writers and readers, speakers and listeners, and teachers of writing. These different ways of being and behaving in school are, initially at least, discovered, then considered, sometimes challenged, even rejected, but most often embraced in the reflective writing that I ask students to do about that experience. I began this chapter with four samples of such writing that I believe, if unpacked, will reveal something about the nature of students' all important experience of these different ways of being and behaving.

"I knew I could trust my audience. . . . I could write."

Most students who enter my English 457 and, I believe, our writing classrooms generally are armed with a formidable *distrust* of the only meaningful audience they have ever had within a school context—their teachers. And why not? Except for the few that have consistently received all "A's" (and even for a few of them), their teachers' responses to their writing, typically very general textual comments followed by a grade, focus on what they should have done or have failed to do. Even when students are given good grades—"A–'s," "B+'s" or "B's"—they are told by the teacher why they didn't receive a better grade: "If only your conclusion had been more comprehensive," they are told. Or, "There is a slight problem with the logical development of your ideas." And so on. As their years of being a student, years of behaving as a writer in a school context, increase, they learn to distrust even their teachers' most effusively positive comments, unless, of course, they see that "A." And then, they even learn to distrust that "A," if their next teacher-examiner does not also give them an "A."

In this English 457 course (as I do in all of the courses I teach), I ask that students keep a reading and writing journal, three to four pages a week of talking-on-paper about their own writing experience, about their responses to what they are reading, and about their small-group activities. Each week then, I read and talk-on-paper back to them. Often, I ask questions. I intend that over time these journals should develop into a kind of written conversation that will allow me to get to know all the students and participate with each of them in a meaningful discussion of them(our)selves as writers and readers and their (our) thoughts about becoming writing teachers. Usually, the students' initial response to this invitation to talk-on-paper to me involves a request for topic—"Well, what are we supposed to write about?" When they turn them in the first few times, either in a brief conversation after class or in the journals themselves, they say, "I hope this was what you were looking for?" And finally, when I return their journal entries to them and they read my responses, particularly the questions that line the margins, they interpret them not as an attempt to begin an authentic exchange, questions begging responses, but either as a kind of indirect faultfinding or as meaningless scratchings without a purpose since they need not either rewrite the particular journal entry or necessarily answer those questions in a future entry. I mention this journal writing and students' responses in order not only to illustrate the depth and seriousness of the distrust that has been engendered in students for their teachers, but to locate in a specific example how unready they truly are to experience themselves as students or as writers apart from the school frame that those traditional conventions have created. Indeed, given the school frame within which both students and teachers most often operate—teachers alone assigning students grades at the end of the semester being one key feature or characteristic—I am often amazed that students actually do engage at all in an authentic written conversation with me. If they are to experience, as James Moffett (1968) has for so long advocated, writing as someone saying something [important] to someone else (10), then they need another context for their writing, a context free at least temporarily of the normal and normative teaching-learning conventions associated with school. I believe that creating that context can begin in their small group, and I hope it will extend itself to include the entire classroom community.

Their small group offers a context within which they can begin to write for someone whom they can trust. But what does it mean to be able to trust one's audience? In order to understand, I'd like to return again to the voices of my students:

> It was always nice to know that. . . . I would be talking about my writing with people I had gotten to know quite well.
>
> —Deb

> It is in small groups that I have begun to feel safe . . . that I have begun to experiment with the information . . . provided in the class. It is through sharing my ideas about something I read, something I wrote, something that bothers me or that I'm interested in that I have become a more active participant . . . .
>
> —Jacque

> Each individual [in a small group] should be encouraged to use their own knowledge and experiences to assist the [other] members in any way they can. . . . I know that I personally started to depend on certain members to provide me with certain types of information like: "How can I clarify this?" or "Help me restructure [that]?" "I need some new ideas." or "How could you rephrase this?"
>
> —Sherry

> I was terrified at first to share my private thoughts and words with other people, but I quickly realized [that] we were all in the same boat and eventually those people—not the drawer, became the secure place to put my writing. We all felt nervous, shy, exposed, and fragile and that is part of what made it easier to open up.
>
> —Jennifer

If small groups are to provide a context within which students can trust one another, that is, if small groups are to offer a true alternative context for writing and learning about writing, they must provide, as these students suggest: (1) a chance for the small-group members to get to know one another; (2) the security and safety each needs in order to be able to risk active participation; (3) a shared involvement in their own and one another's writing, such that they encourage a sense of mutual dependence; and finally, (4) a feeling of community, that the experience of any one of the members is related and relevant to the experience of all the members. However, just as the development of enduring friendships or significant relationships of any kind defy, maybe even actively reject, formulaic simplicity, so does the development of small groups within which trust is a key element. Perhaps the most honest way to suggest how trust does develop in small groups is to tell, or rather to highlight, a few of the stories students have told me about their small groups.

Julie's Story

The members of a small group getting to know one another appears to be a very important feature of their experience—not only because they will be sharing their writing with one another for the rest of the semester, but also because of the peculiar interactive dynamics that each group must establish for itself. Julie writes about the first days of her small group.

> Right off the bat, we [found] something to talk about. We discussed what we thought [this] class would be like, what the teacher would be like. We started establishing trust between the members by exchanging our phone numbers and addresses. We talked about what classes we were taking, who was teaching them, how they were going. We were all education majors, so we talked about . . . how much we hated Teachers College.

Actually, these days, exchanging telephone numbers and addresses is a significant show of trust. Yet, more important things were going on. They were learning who each other was, what their school experiences were, and whether those experiences were at all similar. This led to the members of Julie's small group assuming certain roles. She writes:

> Rick became the comic relief, always having a story to tell about his weekend or how late he got up for class. Chris disclosed a lot about her personal life to us. . . . [B]y the end of the semester, I felt like I knew her family, her boyfriend, the kids she worked with at day care. Kate was the leader. Whenever we got off task [apparently that seemed to happen "quite often," according to Julie], she reminded us of our assignment. She was older than the rest of us, we all looked up to her. [Finally,] I saw my role in small group as a kind of motivator. I was usually the first to volunteer to read my piece or offer suggestions to the others.

Learning about one another, and then developing ways of interacting with one another (predictable roles and small-group participant structures) seemed, according to Julie, to have resulted in "a lot of good materials":

> Each member of the small group would bring in a piece of writing and immediately apologize (i.e., "This is really bad, but here it is"). After hearing the piece, [the other] group members would assure that person that his/her piece was good. We would point out parts of the piece that we liked, or things we didn't understand. We offered each other ideas for additions and revisions. I know, for myself, suggestions from group members resulted in good revisions of my pieces. . . . In [my] small group . . . I found that I trusted my group members' opinions and could take their sugges-

tions as them trying to better my writing, not as them trying to
make me feel stupid.

Julie ends her story about her small group with an evaluation that suggests:

> All in all, our small group developed cohesiveness and established
> trust. . . . We became open in sharing our writing, and I think my
> writing progressed because . . . of my small group members.

Heather's Story

Of course, Heather, a member of a different small group, tells another
story:

> At the beginning of the semester all of us [in the class] were kind
> of leery when we heard, ". . . and you will break up into small
> groups to share your writing." YIKES! What a scary thought. You
> mean someone else [someone other than the teacher] is going to
> read my writing. I thought to myself, "I'm not good at writing . . .
> they might get offended at what I have to say." But then I thought,
> "Hey, if everyone else is going to [share their writing], why not?"

She goes on to say:

> I think Rick eased the class into the mode of reader/responder. At
> first he gave us suggestions [about how to respond], questions we
> could ask each other, but after a couple of weeks we were doing
> pretty good on our own . . . [y]ou could hear [group members] say
> things like "I like the way you integrated (whatever) into your
> story," or "I'd like to know more about (such and such)."

During the first few weeks of small-group work, I do ask that students
"try out" a few alternative ways of responding to each other's writing.
It is certainly awkward—in part because these ways of responding are
unfamiliar to them, but mostly because the responses do not follow
from their own interactive experience with someone else's text. As they
get to know one another, begin to trust sharing their writing with each
other, the need, indeed the felt responsibility, to respond out of their
own experience of another's writing becomes paramount. They discover for themselves what they need to say in response. And, for
Heather and the other writers in her small group, the result was that

> [i]t became very exciting to share my work with someone else just
> to hear what they had to say about it. They [unlike almost all of
> Heather's previous writing teachers] were not there to grade me or
> criticize what I had written. My group shared things and offered
> suggestions, but nobody ever told someone that they had to
> change something in their writing. That was great!

Heather ends her story with an evaluation of her experience:

> It was interesting to read other people's stories and find out more about them. In our group, we learned to trust and respect each other as people. We were not in a big contest with each other to see who could write more, or better, or whatever. We were just . . . people who had an opportunity to share our writing with other people and learn from their knowledge and experience.

I believe that Julie's and Heather's stories reveal in their own way those four characteristics of trust so necessary for successful small writing groups. For Julie's small group, drifting off-task or engaging in small talk about the classes they were taking and their teachers helped them, at least initially, to get to know each other. In Heather's small group, it was actually reading each other's stories that allowed them to learn about one another. For Julie's group, they found the safety and security they needed for active participation in the roles they assumed in their small-group interactions. In Heather's, they found the safety and security they needed in the new ways of responding to the writing of others, ways of responding that assumed a genuine interest on the part of the reader and ownership on the part of the writer. Both stories reveal how much Julie and Heather wanted to bring their writing to their small group. They wanted and needed (because they listened to and used) the responses of the other members. They also wanted to respond to the writing of the other writers. They wanted to help others as they had been helped themselves. Finally, it is clear in the evaluations of their small groups that both Julie and Heather felt a sense of community—Julie in the "cohesiveness and established trust" and Heather in her understanding of herself and her other small-group members as "just people who had the opportunity to share their writing . . . and learn."

**"Without a constant, stable group . . . I don't think
I would have continued to write about [a] subject . . .
I so desperately needed to write about."**

Whenever I begin a new writing class (or a teaching of writing class, or even a linguistics class), I tell the students that we (and that includes me) will be writing several different kinds of things throughout the semester—reading and writing journals, process logs, personal narratives, language/literacy observation studies, responses to the writing of others, perhaps even poems, short stories, or whatever. I also tell them that regardless of the form of writing they choose, they can write about or say anything they want. I did the same in this English 457 class. There was, as there usually is, a collective sigh, so noticeable in fact that a few of the students smiled, a few others giggled. When this happened, I wanted to believe that the collective sigh was a sigh of relief. I know that even though students expect always be told what to write about and how to write about it, they resent it. However, as the semester progressed, some of the students complained (individually in my office or as a group once the subject had been brought up in class) that they were having a hard time thinking of things to say. And I wondered.

I've been a student of language too long to believe that the wellspring of language could ever run dry. Of course, it may be true that every now and then and for some reason or other that well needs priming. But as I reminded them, most of them spend more time talking and listening to others talk than almost anything else (including sleeping). Still, I knew they would not complain if they weren't really experiencing some frustration. When I asked them to tell me more, what they said was very revealing, I thought: "Do you really want us to write about anything we want to write about?" Or, "Is what I'm writing about really what you want?" Even, "How are you going to grade Jacque's poem, or Kristi's letter to her parents, or Maureen's short story?" They wanted to know if I was being straight with them. They wanted to know that when they picked something to write about, I was sincere in my interest (the underlying assumption being that no teacher is ever really interested in what her students write about). And they wanted to know how their own individual expressions of independent thinking and meaning making might relate to what they understood (*still!*) to be the normative teaching-learning conventions of the traditional school frame. Good questions. Real questions. My response was to answer their questions as honestly as I could. But then, in turn, I asked them a question: "Have you ever or would you ever ask questions like these to the members of your small group?" Almost as a chorus they responded: "That's different!" And my response: "In most writing classes, you're absolutely right. Now, what do you think about that?"

Our discussion did not stop with the end of a particular class period. Occasionally, as a whole class, we would discuss what was happening in our small groups. Sometimes we would write about it and read aloud what we had written. However, we more often, even routinely, wondered together why small groups seemed to allow and encourage us to write about what we wanted and needed to write about? I'd like again to return to the voices of my students:

> In [English] 457, we read each other's papers like readers—for content and meaning—and that was one thing that made the class very special. We were all writers sharing our work.
>
> —Kristi

> I'm not saying that teachers should not respond [to student writing], but when you're talking about something as personal as sharing drafts . . . there needs to be some relationship with your readers. . . .
>
> —Deb

If small groups are to provide a context within which students can write about what they want and need to write about, then they must also provide, as these students suggest: (1) readers reading for understanding, and (2) readers who establish a genuine relationship with their writers. Again, I'd like to highlight the story Kristi told me about the way the student-readers/writers came together in her small group, a way rarely experienced by student-writers and teacher-readers.

Kristi's Story

Kristi begins her story of her small group by saying how unfamiliar and not a little scary her first experience in small groups was:

> I guess I'll start at the beginning. Things were kind of weird in Rick's class at first. I was intimidated by the writing load and I didn't know what was expected of me. It was definitely different from anything I had experienced in the past. Things developed slowly. . . . I think Rick sensed our anxiety.

She goes on to say that

> I was in an all female group. It was great! We got along really well even though we were all very different. . . . I can remember some of our first meetings when we didn't know what to say. I can also remember some of our last meetings when we didn't know how to shut up. . . . I think it was so hard at first because we were used to correcting papers, not just reading them. After a semester of being readers [though], we could begin to talk to each other like real people. We could tell each other things like "Wow, that really happened?" "Tell me more!" Or, "Is that what you meant?" [And] "I was confused by this passage." We could be real and honest with each other.

For Kristi, the experience of being a reader and just reading meant learning to be real and honest in her responses to what other members of her small group had written. And, to be real and honest meant responding out of her experience of the particular text. All of her sample questions are responses to the experience that a particular text offered her as a reader: amazement, interest leading to further curiosity, clarifying her understanding, and acknowledging her confusion. However, Kristi learned even more from this experience. She says that she learned about herself as a writer and as a person.

> I feel I really developed as a writer in [English] 457. Before I felt like all I was really good at writing . . . was funny anecdotes. After a few months [actually much quicker than that], I realized that there was a lot going on in my life that I wanted to write about, serious stuff, things that weren't easy or funny. I would kind of ache when I sat down to write because I knew what I wanted to write, but I couldn't do it at first. . . . Today, I know there are things I need to write about and I go over them in my head to keep them alive, until I get a chance to put them down.

Kristi learned that when she, as a writer, has "real people" for readers, readers who are interested in understanding what she has to say, rather than in "correcting" what she has said, she begins to discover all the "serious stuff" that she wants and needs to write about. She learned that as a person, "there was a lot going on in [her] life" and that it became important for her "to go over" and "keep alive" all that was going on until she could get a chance to write about it, to share it with the other members of her small group. Kristi ends with this evaluation of her small-group experience:

> You know, it's really not that complicated what happened. . . . We all just respected and trusted each other as people. We didn't try to take over each other's writing. We just . . . read to read. . . . All in all, I really enjoyed my experience in [English] 457 small group. I think that the environment that was created in the classroom is the key to the success of the class. I hope to create a similar environment in my own classrooms, [an environment] where students can be real and develop into the great writers they can be. That doesn't sound too cheesy, does it?

As a reader and as a writer, as a teacher, as a student of language, I find myself wanting to agree with Kristi that "it's really not all that complicated what happened." Yet, as a student of our current educational system and the normative teaching-learning conventions and practices, I know that it is rare for students in a school context to experience readers reading for understanding and readers with whom, as writers, they can establish a genuine relationship. However, it is not only our educational system and the conventions and practices that now work against the sort of reading and writing experience that Kristi has had; it is the students themselves. Rarely in a school context are students allowed or encouraged to show their writing to other students.

And, if they are allowed to share their writing with each other, rarely are they offered ways of responding that are true alternatives to simply "correcting," or are they offered the time and feedback they need to develop their own ways of responding. At first, "things were kind of weird" for Kristi because she had never before been asked to be a real reader and a real writer. It was hard for her to "know what was expected" because the best way to learn how to be a real reader and a real writer is to experience behaving as a real reader and writer—an experience that she had never had before in a school context. Fortunately, Kristi's small group was able to provide her with the experience she needed. From that experience, then, she was able to develop for herself (with the scaffolding help that regular reflective writing and talking can provide) an understanding of what it means to be a real reader and a real writer. And her understanding, I believe, is quite impressive. For example, she understands that "environment" and the nature of the reading and writing experience created within that environment are crucial. Kristi also understands her goal—that students can "develop into the best writers [and readers] they can be."

What does it mean to develop into the best readers and writers we can be (*all* of us, because we must not separate the learning experience of students and teachers)? According to the "Report of the College Strand" in *The English Coalition Conference: Democracy through Language* (Lloyd-Jones and Lunsford 1989):

> Our aim is to develop students with a high degree of practical and theoretical literacy, whose command of language is exemplary. Such a goal rests on the assumption that the arts of language (reading, writing, speaking, and listening) are social and interactive and that meaning is negotiated and constructed. (25)

The writers of the college report, along with the editors of the overall English Coalition document, believe (as I do) that in order for us to develop both our students *and* ourselves as teachers into the best readers and writers we can be, we need to engage in the "social and interactive" processes that we understand reading and writing, speaking and listening to be. Further, we must through these processes not only foster the negotiating and the constructing of meaning, but encourage, and this is an apparent point of emphasis throughout the Coalition document, a critical awareness of or "conscious theorizing" about all those interactive processes and meaning-making activities (28). I believe that the experience of the above processes and activities is best realized, at least initially, in small groups. I also believe that students' reflective thinking about them is best supported through the writing and reading, speaking and listening in small groups.

**"Small groups are places to try out new ideas, make sense of
old ones, and help others do the same. . . ."**

As members of small groups experience trusting one another, and as
they experience responding to the writing of others and to others responding to their writing as real people, readers and writers reading
and writing for understanding, then they can and do begin to explore
that experience for what it might mean to them. I would like again to
return to the voices of my students. More specifically, I would like to
share some of their reflective writings that reveal both the conscious
theorizing and the ways that this conscious theorizing happens in small
writing groups:

> A lot of sharing goes on in small groups. I think I would even con-
> sider sharing a small-group rule. Members bring their writings and
> read them to the rest of the group and then the group re-
> sponds. . . . [And] responding is very important. The writer needs
> input from the other members, but even more important is how
> those members respond. Another small-group rule is always re-
> spond to what you like first. As a writer, I would rather have some-
> one say to me, "I really like the way you described whatever, but
> I'm not sure why you mentioned it so early in the story," than "You
> mentioned whatever too early in the story." If the person respond-
> ing doesn't respond in a sensitive and positive way, then the writer
> will not be encouraged to work on the piece of writing in the fu-
> ture. I don't mean to say that critical responding does not go on in
> small groups. [But] it is important that members know how to re-
> spond . . . in order to keep the writer writing.
>
> —Jacque

> At the beginning of the semester, Rick was giving us suggestions
> about ways we might respond to each other's writing. . . . [And]
> this was working alright for our group, but we wanted more. One
> of the other students in my group, Jennifer, had written comments
> and questions all over a piece of my writing. . . . It was helpful to
> me as a writer because Jennifer wrote more specific com-
> ments. . . . We discussed as a group Jennifer's responses to my
> writing and whether or not this was something we would all want
> to do for the rest of the semester. We all liked the idea for this new
> way of responding.
>
> —Deb

> Before the class, writing, to me, was very personal—so personal
> that for fear of having someone not like what I wrote or misun-
> derstand the message or get hung up on grammar mistakes, I kept
> my writing hidden in a folder. Not only was it in a folder, but also
> in the back of a desk drawer that was usually locked. Every time I
> wrote I forced myself to write the best thing ever on the first try (I

found out that the best way to write an average or mediocre piece is to force yourself to write a great piece) and when the period was put on the final sentence, I would hurriedly put it in the folder and in the desk and never look at it again. That's how I walked into class on the first day. . . . As the semester went on and reading and responding became more familiar . . . I began to understand what each person [in my small group] was interested in. I learned their strong points and their weak points [as responders]. I knew that some would like one piece more than another. This was an amazing realization for me. I . . . accepted the idea that it was good to have a variety of opinions. Even more amazing was the idea that . . . I could still believe in the quality of my own words . . . make my own choices as a writer. . . . I was just becoming comfortable with the balance of the private and the public that comes with writing.

—Jennifer

There are no easy formulae for responding to the writing of others or responding to others' responses to our writing. Like Jennifer, writing is "very personal" for all of us, as are all our ways of using language. Learning to respond to writing and learning to understand and use the responses of others are both situated and developmental experiences. Jacque, Deb, and Jennifer show just how situated and developmental such learning is.

Jacque had been a journalism major, and a very successful one, before she decided that she wanted an education degree and a teaching certificate. Before she entered my class, Jacque had learned that there were certain and clear rules for writing, and she had learned that these rules, if followed, would realize certain and clear aims or goals. Suddenly, when she entered my classroom, she found herself in a small group where neither those other rules nor those other aims were at all appropriate. She had to think about her situation and the situations of the other writers. She had to think about her own goals for herself as a writer, and she had to learn the goals that the other writers in her small group had for themselves. As is apparent from the first rule of small-group interaction that Jacque formulated, she had come to understand writing and reading as interactive behaviors, and that if either writers or readers are to learn and develop there must be exchange, there must "sharing." Jacque also learned that simply sharing is not enough. She, as a writer, along with the other writers in her small group, needed to want to write more, to continue writing "in the future." She learned that perhaps the best way to "keep a writer writing" is to respond in a "sensitive and positive way." There may be those who disagree with the particular pedagogical approach that Jacque was working out for herself. However, I hope no one misses that Jacque, through her experience in her small group, through her reflecting on and constructing of the meaning of that experience, was indeed generating, creating, a pedagogical approach peculiarly appropriate to the context of the moment. She was consciously theorizing about what it means to be a writer and a reader and how writers and readers should behave in a small-group writing and teaching of writing classroom.

Small groups sharing their writing with one another and learning to respond in a sensitive and positive way to that writing constitute, in my mind, a good beginning to small-writing-group interaction. Still, as Deb and the other members of her small group recognized, "we wanted more." As much as writing courses and the teaching of writing courses are about those social and interactive processes and those meaning-making activities, so, too, are they also about *texts*. Deb found Jennifer's "specific comments" helpful because those comments influenced in a significant way the construction and the final realization of her text. Because Jennifer's comments were text-specific, she influenced Deb's choices as a writer. Deb and the other members of her group had experienced text-specific comments before. For years, teacher-readers had not only been influencing, but determining her textual choices as a writer. Deb and the other members of her small group negotiated the line between influencing and determining those textual choices. They decided that as long as readers' responses were both sensitive and positive, both situated within a relationship with the reader and attempting to help the writer create the best text she can (complications and extensions of Jacque's understanding of sensitive and positive), then "they all liked the idea for this new way of responding." The conscious theorizing here seems to be apparent in the negotiation of the relationship between processes, activities, and texts.

Finally, Jennifer began to think about the roles texts play in the world, or at least in the world of her small group. For Jennifer, texts had always been "very personal," so personal that she had kept them "hidden in a folder . . . in the back of a desk drawer that was usually locked." She was afraid of the particular ways that at least some of her previous teacher-readers had used to find fault with her writing, to reject her texts. Teacher-readers had always been the indisputable authorities concerning texts and typically expressed that authority with grades. However, in Jennifer's small group there were no such authorities. There were only readers with various "interests," readers with "strong points" and "weak points," readers who, because they brought different interpretive perspectives to a text, "would like one piece more than another." Texts became much more or perhaps completely other than mere demonstrations to be evaluated. They became expressions of meaning that in turn became opportunities for social interaction that led to mutual understanding. When her readers did not like what she had written or misunderstood her meaning, she could now ask important discussion-generating questions: "Why didn't you like it?" or "What exactly did you think I was trying to say?" Her readers could feel that through their answers, they were giving her valuable feedback that might influence her choices as a writer. And grammatical mistakes, at least the overwhelming majority of them, could be understood for what they were—unfamiliarity with certain norms of conventional usage. Jennifer could value "a variety of opinions" and "still believe in the quality of her words" because writing and reading texts, talking and listening to others talk about texts became opportunities to engage and participate in authentic and significant conversation. The "balance of the private and the public" began to resemble that same balance Jennifer and the other members of her small-group experience in the give and take of everyday talk.

As a writing teacher, I was very satisfied with the complex nature of the "conscious theorizing" about processes, activities, and texts that was occurring in these and other students' reflective writing. Earlier I suggested that at the beginning of this course, students were as yet unable or unready to hear what I wanted to tell them. However, because of their experience in our workshop classroom and reading, writing, talking, and listening to each other in small groups, they had begun, primarily through their reflective writings, to tell themselves and each other what I wanted them to hear. They had become, in effect, their own teachers. My own role gradually shifted from one of facilitating a particular kind of learning and teaching experience to one of focusing their attention on what they were learning and teaching themselves and each other. Still, I believe that it is *very important* to realize that if, as teachers, we encourage students to become, in a sense, participant-observers of their own learning, to reflect in a serious way on the nature of their learning experience, then we must ourselves be open to the understandings that result. I would like to share what some of the students in this class considered to be the potential problems or shortcomings of small groups in writing and teaching of writing courses:

> By the end of the semester I had really mixed emotions regarding . . . small groups. . . . I feel a small group should be the perfect setting for a vigorous exchange of ideas and experiences and involve equal member participation. The days our group was intact . . . were good days. . . . [However] the most basic shortcoming of our group was a lack of a sense of responsibility of a few of the members. [They] missed class too often. . . . [And] missing even one class period, actually eliminates the benefits of two sessions be-

cause when the member does appear, she is unprepared for the current session and is clueless regarding the previous exchange. . . . I sometimes felt cheated out of the possible rewards derived from a more reliable group.

—Maureen

Although I feel that small groups are something that every person should have a chance to experience, there is a part of small groups that is not as positive as the rest. . . . [W]e were with [one] small group throughout the semester. This allowed us to bond together, however, I never got the [kind of] opportunity [I would have liked] to develop [similar] positive, supportive relationships with the other people in the class.

—Adena

When we started working in small groups, I was pretty happy with the other people that were in my group. . . . This provided me with a sense of security. . . . It turned out, however, to be more of a problem than I expected. Because I was so comfortable with my group, I sometimes didn't feel the need to show much in the way of effort. I knew that the group would understand if I didn't quite get around to writing anything. I knew that they were all my friends. . . . I think I would have been able to learn a lot more if I hadn't got so complacent.

—Rick

As a class at least once during the semester (often more than once and perhaps most often in the small groups themselves), we talked about the peculiar problems of attendance and using small groups. We talked about the possible "trade-offs" involved in "switching" small-group members or creating entirely new small groups. And we talked about motivation—where we (any one or all of us within our own particular circumstances) might find the energy and the time to be the best readers and writers that we could be. We also talked as a class about other problems. We talked about small groups that included an uncooperative and therefore disruptive member. We talked about whether a teacher ought to locate herself within one small group or move between small groups or even remain apart from all the small groups. We even talked about whether if students' learning experiences in workshop classes that used small groups were positive, would this mean that the learning experiences in other classes, most typically face-front kinds of classes, be negative. Or the reverse. Many students were especially interested in discussing discipline. In some of the middle or high school situations they had heard about or knew about firsthand, they were afraid that maintaining a balance between "freedom and chaos" while encouraging small groups might be impossible. We talked about all of the above and more. Some students found the answers they needed. Others did not. Others yet remained noncommittal until they had their own classes. Such is conscious theorizing and the ways conscious theorizing happened in English 457.

"It takes a lot of work, time, and energy, and care. . . ."

I have certain things I want to say about using small groups in writing and reading, talking and listening, and teaching of writing classrooms. The most important way to help students develop a complex, yet contextually responsive understanding of themselves as writers, readers, and teachers of writing, is to offer them, or rather to allow them to offer themselves, the *experience* of being and behaving as all of the above. However, it is not simply experience that I am interested in, but experience of a particular kind. I want students to experience the cohesiveness and established trust that small writing groups are usually fairly effective at providing. I want them to experience being just people availing themselves of the opportunity to share their writing and learning. I want them to experience behaving as real readers and writers, reading and writing for understanding. I want them to experience the relationships that develop when they collectively engage one another in the social and interactive processes we know reading, writing, talking, and listening to be. I want them to experience for themselves and attend to the experience of others as they all make meaning with language. And, I want them to experience thinking and then writing and reading and talking and listening about the meaning that they all have experienced making. Finally I want them to experience the work, time, energy, and care it will take to provide like experiences for their future students.

I do not believe that the traditional classroom teaching-learning conventions offer either the particular kind of experience or the opportunity to reflect on the nature of that experience from which our students or we as teachers can grow. Still, I am not intent on reformation, on reforming a current composition paradigm, or revolution, on promoting a paradigm shift. Rather, I am interested in transformation. I am interested in facilitating the kind of experience that allows students and teachers to be and to behave as writers, readers, speakers, listeners, and thinkers, *and* most importantly, to announce themselves as such with a "certain joy" and "common spirit" that keeps them writing, reading, speaking, listening, and thinking (Jones 1991, 265). I believe small writing groups can help to realize such an aim.

7 A Conversation about Small Groups

Ruth Mirtz
Florida State University

In this chapter, I'll start where Robert, Rick, and I think you, our readers, are: in the middle of a course, planning a course, wondering why you bought this book, more certain or more confused about what you know about small groups. Just as we try to remember to start where our students are, rather than where we as teachers are, I'll try to begin with immediate questions and specific problems that trouble the people the three of us have talked to about small groups, rather than the types of narratives or descriptions with which we've structured most of this book.

Q: I've read this whole book, and I still am not sure I understand the goals of small-group work in a writing class. How do you rationalize the amount of time spent in small groups in a class that ultimately seeks to improve students' writing, not their oral behavior?

A: What we do and say is largely determined by who we are, who we think we are, who we are trying to be, who we wish we were. Many of these "identity" factors take on a presence in written or spoken discourse. The need for constant direct dialogue in a writing class comes partly from the needs of writers who are trying to construct texts which simultaneously express their selves and relate to other selves, within or without. The second, but no less important, reason is that real learning takes place when one comes to understand the requirements of the role as writer, tries on new roles as writer and reader, and develops meaningfully coordinated or cooperative roles as writer, reader, friend, authority, and whatever else is needed.

Students will translate the difficulties they have finding a workable, comfortable role within our courses into like or dislike for their group members or instructor, feelings of injustice about requirements and evaluations in the course, and so on. They are accustomed to seeing their maturing and learning process (what they often call "real-world learning") as something separate from classroom or academic work.

The transformation that occurs when we see small groups and the writing process as sites of struggles among roles is that students' ability to write and respond well becomes intimately tied to their ability to resolve conflicts and to communicate with group members effectively; that ability is dynamic, constantly changing and adjusting to new situations and ideas. We change how we teach writing by incorporating the whole dimension of small-group dynamics into what we already teach about the process of inventing, revising, and responding.

These goals are the two most important ones for small groups in writing classes for us. Many times, however, small groups are more or less opportunities for (1) getting to know each other and sharing experiences; (2) warming up and reminding students of recent discussions; (3) refocusing the class on questions and issues larger than individual assignments; (4) generating more ideas and reactions faster than a large group; (5) individualizing instruction, especially participation in discussion; and (6) encouraging exposure to diverse perspectives and cultures. All six (certainly not an exhaustive list) subgoals are still sites of the struggles among the roles students take on in writing classes.

Q: I'm confused—your talk about small-group behavior keeps turning into a discussion about response to writing.

A: Because we use small groups in our writing class primarily as a way to get more direct, relevant, and quick response to students writing, the small-group behavior we are most interested in is that which helps the response become increasingly effective for all the writers' roles students take on in our classes. Also, the structure and guidelines we set up to help small groups get along are basically response rules. Essentially, we believe nearly all small-group behavior in writing classrooms *is* a response to writing.

Q: I think the small groups in my classes don't work well together because of personality conflicts. If I could find a way to arrange the groups with the right people and personalities together, maybe all the small groups in my class would "work."

A: Personality differences do cause conflicts, but they don't keep us from working together in all sorts of strange situations in the world outside the classroom. Because of the power we have as teachers to move students in and out of groups, we naturally want a way (give

Meyers-Briggs tests, for instance) to find out who would get along best with which others.

Outside the classroom, however, one can generally choose the personalities one wants to avoid; students can't do that, short of ignoring a member of their small group. One student may have an overbearing, excessively confrontational way of talking to strangers, while the other students in her group are uncomfortable or even unable to see this student's behavior as valuable. The others may consider her behavior impolite or downright rude. This group is likely to stop responding all together and will certainly have difficulties unless one of the quieter students takes a stronger leadership role and balances the more aggressive personality.

It seems cruel to leave such a group intact, but in our experience, changing groups in order to find compatible personalities only causes a different set of problems. A group with very similar interests and ways of handling communication will often fall into the habit of chatting about their writing instead of responding toward significant revision.

All groups have differences and conflicts, many of which are well below the surface of the conversation and the responding you may observe or participate in. Many of us were taught from childhood to avoid talking about small-group behavior, to not question a group member's words, so even instructors, as members of a group, find that they need more conflict-resolution skills.

Q: Then what do I actually do with a small group which doesn't get along?

A: Ideally, a small group with conflicts which interfere with their ability to respond helpfully to each other's writing will find a way to work through the problems. Realistically, they will need help from their instructor, either in the form of modeling or self-monitoring.

(1) Modeling: the instructor becomes an active part of the group and shows students better ways to handle conflicts, such as asking outright about differences of opinion: "We seem to be disagreeing on this. What shall we do?" or "Since we can't seem to agree on this, let's use one of the guidelines from Tuesday." Most students respond to humor and know how to use humor to break tension. Instructors can show students how they use humor to lighten a conflict while not burying the conflict at the same time ("Gee, if we had some boxing gloves, we could take this outside and settle it like real men").

(2) Self-monitoring: The instructor can ask a small group to write letters to each other about how the group is going and what they'd like to do differently. By focusing on what other things the group could do or on creative alternatives, negative reactions about the current situation can be diplomatically left out. Reading different versions of what the small group seems to be doing in general ("Describe your small group") can be enlightening for students who don't realize how their behavior is being interpreted and perhaps completely misunderstood. An especially shy student is sometimes perceived as uninterested or indifferent when she is actually desperately trying to get a word into the conversation.

Q: You never directly intervene in a small group?

A: Of course, there are extreme cases when one member is simply out of line, refuses to try to cooperate, and is making everyone completely miserable. So there is a third method for dealing with conflicts:

(3) Intervention: Sometimes the instructor simply needs to take over the leadership of a group and spend significant amounts of time in one group (and simply hope that the other groups will function sufficiently in the interim). Some groups enjoy being labeled the "problem group" or the "slow group" because they garner attention and have a group identity provided for them. Other groups may resent the extra attention the instructor gives one group, but doing a little "floating" during each workshop allows you to explain that some groups need more help than others. Students are generally very alert to what's going on in other groups—they know, for instance, when one group is louder or quieter than other groups, when one group loses members regularly, and so on. If the instructor assumes that all groups have problems from time to time, then she will be talking to the class as a whole regularly about the problems small groups have and how to deal with them.

In rare cases, a student needs to be pulled aside and persuaded individually to resist certain ingrained communication habits, such as incessant teasing and joking or hostile, negative comments. However, giving one of these students the option of not participating in a group is not a good recourse, either, even though a terribly tempting one. This student is exactly the student who needs the time and attention paid to her small-group behavior; if the instructor lets her off the hook, the student's next instructor will merely get the task.

Q: So it really doesn't matter what method I use to form the small groups?

A: We truly suspect that we are overly concerned about how to form small groups. Whether one decides to let the students form their own groups, counts off, or uses some logical device to match or complement students doesn't seem to matter all that much. With any method, in any class, some small groups will work independently and need little modeling or monitoring, and some small groups will need intense attention and help from the instructor. No method that we have heard of will ensure perfectly formed small groups. An instructor should use the method which she is comfortable with, seems fair, and fits in the time frame and flexibility of her plans for the class. For instance, if you want to form small groups on the first day of class, you don't have time to get to know the students, and you may not even have the extra two or three minutes it takes for students to form their own groups; therefore, you'll choose a quick and easy way to form groups.

Q: Your definition of a "good" small group seems to be different than mine. I think a small group works well when they focus on drafts and follow the instructor's instructions; a small group doesn't work when they don't talk, finish early, and use their own ways of organizing themselves and responding to drafts.

A: The way we define our small groups as "working" is unusual. Actually, we are constantly reexamining our definition of a "working" small group (or a "good" small group) within the context of small groups in general. We often worry that a small group isn't "working" because they aren't obediently following directions or because they don't seem to care much for each other, and yet we see those students improving their writing as often and as much as the students in groups that do seem to value each other's writing and enjoy each other's company. What's going on?

"On-task" behavior is a trap, we have found, and just as problematic as defining a "good" student as one who plays our games according to our rules. What appears to be on-task or off-task is often the opposite; what students are learning is more important to us than whether they follow our instructions to the letter. Some groups need larger amounts of seemingly "off-task" talk in order to respond meaningfully to texts. They'll start off talking about the game on Saturday, their plans for the weekend, and half the class period will be gone before they start looking at their drafts. We don't usually worry about this form of procrastination early in the term because it helps students learn about each other, find out what interests other group members, and in general relaxes them enough to be able later to respond helpfully. They'll be the group that can look at one member's draft and make suggestions based on other stories they know the member has stored away or other talents the member has. They will be able to truly "re-envision" their texts and may sometimes have problems deciding which revisions to make and when to stop revising.

The group that seems to be made of "good students" will launch immediately into following exactly the instructions given to them, but suffer from superficial or irrelevant response because they don't know each other well enough to respond helpfully. They will be the group that gives advice too soon rather than response and reactions. They will quickly tire of the responding guidelines, and because they can't use much of the advice they get from their small group, they will rely on the instructor's response solely. They need, as much as the "off-task" group does, to monitor their group behavior and talk about how their group is functioning effectively and not so effectively.

One the most frustrating aspects of using small groups in composition classrooms is their tendency to come up with their own ways of dealing with things. Sometimes the instructor needs to remind them of the guidelines and instructions because they really are trying to take the easy way out, while other groups are negotiating an effective way to proceed and process their own conflicts. Some groups need monitoring, but not necessarily interference.

We need to constantly examine our own definition of "working" when we talk about small groups: Do we mean following instructions, or working out differences, or helping to improve their writing, or discovering how other writers work, or experimenting with their identity as a writer?

Q: Don't all small groups go through a certain process during the semester? Shouldn't they get through these conflicts as soon as possible and then move on to the real work of the small group? Shouldn't the teacher's job be to push each group through the process as quickly as possible so that they can start working on their texts?

A: We often talk about how we deal somewhat differently with small groups early in the term than at midterm or toward the end of the term. The first few week of class are a time when students need more time to get to know each other, find out how each other thinks and acts, and develop functional ways of getting along despite the inevitable conflicts. By midterm, group members should be well-acquainted and ready for more difficult responding and reading tasks, ready to take more risks and experiment more boldly. By the end of term, we hope that all of our students have a rich repertoire of responding and con-flict-resolution strategies that will prepare them for any other small-group experiences they have the rest of their lives.

Did you notice how conditional and wishful the last two sentences were? We can be fairly certain about what all students need during the first two or three weeks of class—structure, guidelines, time to get ac-quainted. But after that, each small group must be treated individually. There are no other reliable "phases" a group will go through, although happily, many groups do follow the process of development (described above). A great deal of social science research is devoted to determin-ing the possible processes and consequently has come up with elabo-rate theories with fancy diagrams. Whenever we have tried to apply these theories of processes to our students, we find the actual processes much messier, more recursive, and ultimately not much help.

We stress monitoring and modeling all semester, because a small group continues to be a dynamic, constantly renegotiating location for students all semester. Some traditional-age students seem to have less tolerance for stability and routine than older adults and will work at destabilizing some small aspect of the group as soon as they feel bored. And when one student brings a much more personal draft than she has ever brought before (or much more political draft or a draft which re-sponds to another student's draft), the small group must change its ways of responding to be sensitive to the needs of the writer's experi-ment. Some students are much less sure of their own identities and will need room and space to try out new roles. The student who leads con-fidently one week may be completely silent the next week. A group which launches into wonderfully directed response to texts one week may need half the class period the next week to talk out and rediscover themselves as peers and friends.

The constant renegotiating that takes place in all groups is what keeps many nonacademic study groups or support groups going for years. The same need makes it difficult for students to change groups during the school term and is why we suggest not changing groups during a normal fifteen- or sixteen-week semester course.

Q: So I shouldn't change the small groups at all during the term?

A: Inevitably we end up moving some members of small groups, but we don't tend to change the groups simply for variety or convenience or because students say they are bored. I often end up shuffling some members the very first day of class, before the students introduce them-selves, in order to balance out the number of men and women. When I can avoid it easily, I prefer to have either groups of all women, all men, or two men with two women. The group I try to avoid is the group with a three-to-one ratio, which sometimes places a student at a disadvantage. That's one change I can make easily because I can identify the sexes easily (most of the time). Any other special needs or compatibilities are impossible to learn reliably during the first days of class.

I also change groups to keep the numbers even—three or four in each group. If enrollment changes because of drops or adds, then the small groups may have to be adjusted, but I try to warn students on the first day of class that the possibility exists.

We structure our classes so that there are many opportunities for all the students to meet and work with students besides those in their small groups, even though they may workshop their drafts and papers with the same small group all semester. Our students tell us that they enjoy working with students outside of their small group, but that they feel much more comfortable responding to drafts with a stable long-term group.

Q: What about gender differences? If one of my small groups consists of all women, they inevitably become a support group while my groups of all men become very competitive in appearing "cool" while rebellious.

A: We don't find a support group or a "cool" group as much of a problem as a group which consistently leaves one voice unheard or causes a member too much discomfort to be learning at the same time. Rather than add too many requirements to the ideal group makeup, we work with those groups who have found a real, workable group identity for themselves, to turn that "cool guy" attitude into "cool writer" attitude, or to push the support group to get past its unconditional encouragement. They are not groups in conflict as much as groups with too limited an idea of what their group can be. When we are participating in those groups, the knowledge we point out about their group problems is part of what we are making deliberate, articulate, and changeable in their group behavior.

Q: Even when I have small groups with exactly the same number of members, one group always finishes early. What do I do with them?

A: It may depend on just how early they are finishing. If a group finishes five or six minutes before the other groups, that seems a reasonable amount of time to leave them to their own conversation. Five extra minutes of getting acquainted, especially if the group members didn't pause for socializing before getting started, can only help most groups.

More than five minutes is a good time for a small group to do some writing. An excellent short writing assignment, which I often make a general rule for groups (and which sometimes ensures that they will stretch their responding time in order to finish with the other groups and avoid the extra writing) is to report on what happened in their small group. They might also start writing in their journals for the next entry, either on a suggested topic or on one of their own inspiration.

A group which consistently finishes fifteen or more minutes early needs closer monitoring. They may simply be incredibly efficient, they may have brought spectacularly short texts, or they may be completely lost about how to respond to each other's texts and not really exchanging reactions and ideas. Because my presence as a fellow writer always tends to slow down a group, I often choose to become a part-time member of the group that always finishes too early. And I often say things to them like "Are you sure that's all we can help you with?" or "But you didn't say why you thought the ending was good." I often become the social leader of those groups, too, because sometimes the quick finishers are the group of four, shy nontalkers, and they need someone to engage them in conversation.

I think it's important not to "punish" small groups which finish early with the equivalent of "seat work" or expect them to sit there doing nothing, waiting for the other groups. On the other hand, I prefer not to let them leave early either, choosing rather to find a fruitful additional activity which helps them monitor themselves and their group or by modeling the kind of responding which does take time and energy.

Q: What about using small groups not only for workshopping on drafts but for collaborating on group-authored texts or for discussing assigned reading from imaginative or professional writing?

A: We find that the joys and pains of small groups responding to drafts are the same for other kinds of small groups. However, the roles students struggle with change when the goals of the group change. In a collaborative group, more unity is needed in how texts should be written—that is, more of the group members will be forced to take on unfamiliar writerly roles. In a discussion group, the status of the text is often more of a problem, causing students to work out their roles as mass reader or aesthetic critic, for example.

Q: I always thought putting students into small groups was a great way to reduce the load on the teacher.

A: Small groups can reduce the role of the teacher as an absolute authoritarian and can eliminate the need for students to write for a murky "general audience." However, using small groups in a composition class is a tremendous amount of work if the instructor intends for the groups to work as circles of fellow writers and readers.

Some teachers do use the time to mark papers or read the newspaper, but that is not a role which will ensure that the small groups will be successful. We strongly advocate an active role for the instructor during small-group workshops, either as a floating member or as a permanent member of one group. Even then, it often seems (especially to administrators) as though a teacher isn't doing anything when the small groups are meeting during class.

The instructor is constantly monitoring the groups, trying to be in at least two groups during each class session and often speaking in general with all the groups. Sometimes she will sit in on one group while listening to another group nearby. She has to make sure that each group finishes at about the same time. A group which finishes early needs an extra assignment. A group which never finishes on time needs to be pushed to either elect a timekeeper each week or become more aware of the amount of nonessential talking they do. The instructor reads, in addition to the drafts and final papers of each students, reports from each student about the small group and often responds to those additional reports. The instructor is also a fellow writer, and in that role, spends extra time each week keeping her own writing journal or notebook and drafting texts to share with the class. She also disciplines herself to read published texts and recent research in regard not only to composition, but also to small-group behavior and small-group pedagogy.

For some of us, small groups became a pedagogical method when we sought to individualize our instruction more and allow students more self-paced learning. A small group allows a student to work on her own projects at her own speed while still getting the exposure (and some mild pressure) from other students working at different levels and paces. Such individualizing of our instruction takes enormous amounts of time. First, we must keep close track of anywhere from 30 to 100 (or more) students' work separately and also counsel their choices. Then, we must find ways to draw all these separate learners together with issues which most of them have in common, although in many different ways. After more than a decade of teaching, I still find this task overwhelming.

Q: Now you've made it sound like too much work.

A: It's actually a different kind of work than most of us are accustomed to. It's also, fortunately, the kind of work that keeps us challenged as learners ourselves and provoked as teachers. The modeling we do in small groups as expert small-group members keeps us on our toes, because while we can read about research on small groups (or conduct our own), and we can predict what our small groups will do, we are usually called on to model and problem-solve on the spot, as the conflicts come up. When we join the small groups as fellow but expert writers, we get a chance to practice our own craft, to consider ourselves writers for a while.

   So if it turns out to be more work, it's the kind of more work we need in order to be good teachers. Not more paperwork or grading, but more interaction with students which lets us learn more about them and about writing and learning processes.

Q: But there's so much to do already in my class, and now I have so many ideas about small-group work. It's the middle of the semester and I've already set out my goals and evaluation process. Where do I start?

A: We agree that an instructor shouldn't, under normal circumstances, suddenly make wholesale changes in a course because a better idea comes along in midstream. But we do hope you start making plans for next semester.

   If you have never used small groups or haven't in a while and would like to try a limited experiment at any point in the semester, then here's a suggestion: Begin with a tightly focused, very specific writing and sharing activity which correlates with something your class has been discussing or working on, and ask the students to write an informal description of their writing process on the current assignment. Form small groups to read the descriptions out loud to each other with the rules of no apologies from the writers and no criticism from the listeners. Give the groups time to read out loud and talk about the similarities and differences between the descriptions. Then follow up by asking students to write from three to five minutes about what happened in their small group, to be handed in to you.

   The more specific the tasks you give to the groups and the more naturally you can assume they will have no problem with this exercise, the more "in control" and relaxed you may feel. The follow-up responses will let you know what happened and how to adapt your instructions and expectations for the next small-group activity.

Q: Sometimes I think my students don't work well in small-groups workshops because they just don't know how to work in small groups, in general. They should learn these skills in high school. Why do I have to teach them?

A: If our students came to us with no skills in small-group work, we would have written a much different book. Instead, our students come as seasoned small-group members of a different kind: they've been active in groups of friends of various sizes, clubs and committees, lab partners, and families. Those groups have provided both positive and negative experiences, though, and we draw on both kinds in college writing classes. Students don't need training in small-group behavior; they need to learn how to reapply what they already know about themselves and how they relate to people in a writing class.

Q: I've had some pretty uncomfortable experiences in small groups, myself. And I was trained to work individually and competitively as a graduate student and as a teacher. Aren't I the least likely person to make small-group work succeed in my classroom?

A: On the contrary, you are probably more sensitive to the level of comfort and discomfort your students are experiencing. For good or ill, instructors take all their educational baggage with them into the classroom. By being aware of the influence of your past experiences, you are well on the way to understanding how you want small groups to work in your own classroom. Plus, you've got some stories about how you don't think small groups should work to tell your students, who can (and should) always regale you with theirs.

Q: I'd like to find out more about small groups. What other books do you suggest?

A: We hope you will first attempt to learn more about small groups from the best source: the small groups in your classroom. Take a few notes while participating in a group. Collect and analyze the short reports your students write about how their small group is going. Look for the metaphors or other kinds of language they use to describe their group. Tape-record one small group which you aren't participating in and promise not to listen to it until after the semester is over—then *do listen to it*. See also the recommended readings in the appendix of this book.

Q: All these practical matters aside, don't you have a social agenda of some kind behind this small-group pedagogy?

A: Like most people, we don't align ourselves with any one social policy or political group. We have been influenced by such diverse thinkers as Paulo Freire, Ann Berthoff, Erving Goffman, Thomas Kuhn, the Sophists of ancient Greece, although we have probably been influenced most about small groups by the thousands of students who told us about what happened in our classrooms. We believe that both individual autonomy and interaction in groups, large and small, are necessary for developing our students' writing processes and facility, as well as their critical acumen and their sense of responsibility toward both themselves and others.

   If we were to say we have a social agenda, then it would be the need for society to provide better education for all segments of that society. We believe that small groups are a part of that better education under conditions of equality and opportunity.

8 Exhortation: Beyond the Small Group—Personal, Pedagogical, and Professional Lives

Robert Brooke
University of Nebraska–Lincoln

Ruth Mirtz
Florida State University

Rick Evans
University of Nebraska–Lincoln

The semester is over and I'm looking at the computer printout of my students' evaluation of me as their instructor. The numbers again seem too low, certainly lower than the departmental average. Sitting on my desk is a stack of student-written responses about their small groups, all positive and articulate about what they learned from being in a small group. I remind myself that 50 percent of the students' class time is spent in small groups, and no question on the computerized evaluations are about small groups or peer influence. Once again, I write in my required response to these evaluations a description of the difference between the goals of my class and the kind of class tested by the evaluation. Once again, I consider stapling to my response the sheaf of handwritten responses from my students. . . .

Two writing instructors are standing in the stairway, talking across the banisters. One is describing a student who was doing marvelously in her class and was generally the leader of her small group. Suddenly and inexplicably, the student disappeared from class. Against her usual inclination, the instructor decided to try and call her, but no one answered the telephone; none of the other students had seen her. The worst-case scenarios run, unspoken, through their heads.

A friend, a part-time adjunct professor, tells me this story after a long day: "I had a precious thirty minutes after a class and before a committee meeting to read the notes my students wrote to me about their small group. I sat down to read the stack of pages, and a book representative stopped by to chat. Then, a student from three years back knocked on the door, wanting a folder so far buried in a stack of student work that I imagined telling her that I tossed it. Then the telephone rang; it's one of the committee members asking for a list of people who might be interested in judging a high school writing contest, and oh, if I have notes from the last committee meeting, could I bring them along? Finally, I locked my door, turned out the light, unplugged the telephone, and read three of the notes from my students by the light of the window before I had to leave."

—Excerpts from Ruth Mirtz's
teaching journal

More than our classrooms change when we use small groups as a teaching method or mode or philosophy. We can no longer see our classes as merely another section or two of competently taught composition. The stories above illustrate how institutional processes put in place around our classrooms are designed for teacher-talk, imposed knowledge, and blank-slate students. Anne Ruggles Gere (1987) points out that even though the history of small groups extends back at least two centuries, "the continuing 'discovery' of them demonstrates the extent to which they have remained on the edges of educational consciousness" (52).

Once we've used small groups in our classrooms for any length of time, we find that we know our students in new ways, we prioritize our professional tasks differently, and we resist traditional assumptions of teacher performance. When we want to use small groups to their fullest potential, we have to change more than our pedagogical ideas and classroom management skills: we also have to find ways to work around, adapt, translate, and mediate those surrounding structures of programs, requirements, evaluations, and administration, until meaningful change is possible in those areas, too.

Our professional lives are implicated in our commitment to small groups. In a recent article, Jane Tompkins (1992) writes of the need for academe to become more cooperative in general, to combat the forces in higher education that seek to isolate professors and students in endless hierarchical competition. Describing her early career as an adjunct professor in a large city university, she writes:

Things could have been a lot better if we in the university had been accustomed to attending to the quality of our lives as members of a group, if we had taken time to consider what makes people feel valued and cared for. But there was no attempt. It would have been regarded as unintellectual and a frill. (17)

She writes of feelings of isolation inherent in university life, and of the disdain with which "The Profession" looks at concerns for "community" and "collaboration" (two of the key words for composition teachers committed to small groups). Because of its emphasis on individual accomplishment, the structure of higher education actually works against companionship, community, and real interchange between teachers or scholars or the possible existence of a teacher-scholar. Feeling the pressure of individual accomplishment, instructors find themselves closing their office doors, working at home, avoiding extensive contact with students or difficult committee work—we find ourselves, in short, avoiding real interaction with those who surround us in our intellectual communities. Such isolation is endemic in academe and affects our contact with the world outside of academe as well. bell hooks (1989), a feminist writer and scholar, describes an alienation among many African American scholars when they are successful in academe. Talking and writing from any narrow perspective, hooks says, "alienates most folks who are not also academically trained and reinforces the notion that the academic world is separate from real life, that everyday world where we constantly adjust our language and behavior to meet diverse needs" (78). Ira Shor (1987), a proponent of liberatory pedagogy, calls this position of isolation the "academic pedestal" to which some of us aspire and from which some of us are barred (84). Like Tompkins, hooks, and Shor, we see the need for higher education to change, to become a place which "models social as well as personal achievement," to show through its structures and actions our need to work together, negotiate disagreements, and support each other in the true interdependence of intellectual life. Our experience in small groups, both with our students and with each other, demonstrates to us again and again the imperative for such meaningful change. Both hooks and Shor remind us to focus on our everyday world, especially the everyday world of students, lesson plans, and committee meetings. We must be "ever vigilant," says hooks. "It is important to know who we are speaking to, who we most want to hear us, who we most long to move, motivate, and touch with our words" (78).

Touching others with our words and making meaningful change through those words doesn't come out of nowhere. We are sometimes impatient with our students who complain that they know they need to revise their paper but they don't know where to start. "Start anywhere," we say, "anywhere, as long as you're thinking and re-envisioning your ideas and experiences and means of expression." We are equally impatient with ourselves for complaining too often that our colleagues and administrators and students don't understand what we're doing in our classrooms, with small groups or workshops, with whatever new and not-quite-articulated idea we're exploring.

So we end this book with a plea to you as well as to ourselves: *Start anywhere!*

Observe small groups in every context, especially in your own classrooms. Visit other classrooms and invite peers to visit yours. Ask students what they think. Support your peers and students for what seems sensible to you.

Question what happens, what connects, what conflicts. Write your questions and answers and read others' questions and answers. Join local or national composition groups and find out what others are doing and thinking. Introduce yourself and talk to speakers whose work you admire. Write letters to writers whose ideas make sense to you and engage them in dialogue. Use your electronic mail.

Organize students, co-workers, friends. Volunteer to lead a brown-bag lunch group. Ask to serve on committees which have evaluative or planning power. Support colleagues and administrators who are pursuing or exploring goals you find useful.

Start anywhere. The observing, questioning, and organizing spurs thinking, re-envisioning, and writing. It sparks discussion of ideas and policies in small groups, classrooms, teachers, universities. It contributes to our awareness of the real interdependence of professional, personal, and pedagogical life, and perhaps in the long run to the real development of an intellectual community (which, after all, is what the word *college* originally meant). If small groups bring the world into our classrooms through the inclusion of students' own thoughts, emotions, and agendas, they also force our classrooms back into the world again, back into the professional and personal contexts which surround our lives as teachers. We could ignore, deny, keep to ourselves the return of our classrooms into this larger life, but instead we must lead it. We can't afford not to see small groups as a site of educational change for all students, not just in the way they see their relationship to their writing, but in the whole context of life in the world.

Appendix:
Recommended Readings

The following readings are ones we've learned from in developing our own uses of small groups in the writing classroom. We consider these "must-read" sources—sources with which every teacher using small groups should try to be familiar. Many other interesting but less crucial sources are listed in the works cited listing (following this appendix), if you find yourself interested in some particular aspect of small groups and would like to learn more.

We've organized our recommended readings around three headings: *Motivating Effective Response, Understanding Small-Group Processes,* and *Background Theory.*

Motivating Effective Response

Calkins, Lucy McCormick. 1986. "Writing Conferences." In *The Art of Teaching Writing,* 117–59. Portsmouth, NH: Heinemann.

This wonderful resource describes the basic strategies Calkins uses to help elementary school children gain control over the processes of responding to their own and others' texts. Since, as she says, these strategies aren't natural to young children but must be taught, she provides a framework for thinking about response pedagogically that is both fundamental and elegant. Teachers and writers of all levels, kindergarten through graduate school, can learn from her division of response into five separate types of conferences: content (focused on meaning), design (focused on form), process (focused on the strategies and tempos of writing), evaluation (focused on quality and development), and editing (focused on error identification). For each type of conference, she provides strategies for conducting such inquiry privately by yourself on your own writing, in one-on-one tutorials, and in small peer groups. Like Elbow's text, her section is a wonderful resource for both students and teachers.

Elbow, Peter. 1981. "Feedback." In *Writing with Power: Techniques for Mastering the Writing Process,* 237–77. New York: Oxford University Press.

This section of Peter Elbow's manual for writers provides the best introduction we know to the kinds of questions writers can use to get response from readers. Elbow distinguishes between criteria-based feedback (response which evaluates the text in comparison to ideal texts of that genre in the reader's past experience) and reader-based feedback (response that describes the reader's emotional, physical, and intellectual reaction to the piece during the process of reading), and explains the different times these two kinds of response are useful. He then provides lists of possible questions to elicit each type of response. For criteria-based feedback, he provides twenty-four potential questions, including such evaluative prompts as: "Is the whole thing unified? Is there one central idea to which everything pertains? Or is it pulling in two or three directions?"; "Does the diction, mood, or level of formality fit the audience and occasion?"; and "Is the basic idea or insight a good one?" For reader-based response (which he considers the more important kind of response, as do we), he provides forty-one possible questions, including such descriptive prompts as: "What was happening to you, moment by moment, as you were reading this piece of writing?"; "Summarize what you feel the writer is trying but not quite managing to say. Where is the writing trying to go—perhaps against the writer's will?"; and "Make up an image for the relationship between the writer and reader. Does the writer seem to have his arm draped familiarly over your shoulder? Is the writer shouting from a cliff to a crowd below? Sending a letter bomb?" In our experience with small groups, we've found Elbow's lists of questions an important resource, both for ourselves and for our students.

Thomas, Dene, and Gordon Thomas. 1989. "The Use of Rogerian Reflection in Small-Group Writing Conferences." In *Writing and Response: Theory, Practice, and Research*, edited by Chris M. Anson, 114–26. Urbana: National Council of Teachers of English.

This short article highlights and explains one of the most consistent features of successful group response: groups who support each other's writing without criticizing and who spend time exploring each writer's developing meaning usually succeed beautifully. The Thomases connect these features of response to Rogerian methods of reflection in therapy, showing that the simple act of describing back to the writer what you, as reader, believe they meant by what they wrote provides all the essential response a writer needs. Such response brings out clearly where a text is succeeding in conveying a message, where a text is creating alternative messages it didn't intend, and where a writer is unsure of the message she is trying to convey.

Understanding Small-Group Processes

Bormann, Ernest. 1975. "Cohesiveness and the Task-Oriented Group" and "The Social Climate of Groups." Chapters 7 and 8 in *Discussion and Group Methods: Theory and Practice*, 141–97. 2nd ed. New York: Harper & Row.

These two chapters of Bormann's textbook for undergraduate speech communication students give a clear and readable summary of Bormann's extensive research at the University of Minnesota into what we've called the task/maintenance division in group processes. Since that concept has proved useful, both for our thinking and for students' own reflection on their groups, we believe that teachers ought to be familiar with its sources. Bormann's bibliography provides follow-up research sources for those who are interested.

Elbow, Peter. 1973. "The Teacherless Writing Class." In *Writing without Teachers*, 76–146. New York: Oxford University Press.

This, for us, is *the* book on small-group processes which teachers should start out reading. Written explicitly for writers who want to form a writing group without the interference of teachers, this book sets forth some important strategies for making peer groups work and identifies the most likely problems groups will encounter. Central to Elbow's notion of groups is the idea that everyone needs to make a commitment to continuing his or her writing—and this commitment requires that all writers bring writing to each meeting—and that anyone can wreck the group if he or she wants to. His wonderful section on "How to Destroy the Group Secretly" is an especially useful section for teachers' and students' reflection on group problems. This is the book each of us read first in our journey toward small-group writing classes.

Rothwell, Dan. 1992. "Periodic Phases of Group Development." In *In Mixed Company: Small-Group Communication*, 55–79. New York: Harcourt Brace Jovanovich.

This section of Rothwell's recent textbook is a most readable account of the other idea we've borrowed from the speech communication literature as an aid for helping students reflect on their small groups: the idea of the forming, storming, norming, and performing sequence to group interaction. Using these stages as reflective devices often helps groups identify potential issues they need to work out in their interaction—although we would advise against using the stages as a strict model of necessary progression in groups. Actual group processes are much more complex than these stages suggest—which is why journals like

Small-Group Processes continue to flourish in our sister discipline of speech communication.

Spear, Karen. 1988. *Sharing Writing: Peer-Response Groups in English Classes*. Portsmouth, NH: Boynton/Cook-Heinemann.

This wonderful book is the one we would have written if our classes were aimed at the writing of standard academic essays instead of the wider goal of writing throughout a writer's life. Spear gives useful descriptions of the problems students face as they try to talk about academic essays with each other and sensible advice for helping them become trusting, critical readers of each other's academic efforts. We see this book as a useful companion to our own for teachers working in academic settings.

Background Theory

Elbow, Peter. 1991. "Reflections on Academic Discourse: How It Relates to Freshmen and Colleagues." *College English* 53 (February: 135–55.

Belenky, Mary Field, Blythe McVicker Clinchy, Nancy Rule Goldberger, and Jill Mattuck Tarule. 1986. "Connected Teaching." In *Women's Ways of Knowing: The Development of Self, Mind, and Voice*, 216–29. New York: Basic Books.

The Elbow article is a straightforward and clear presentation of the idea of writing education for life practice, instead of the narrower goal of academic writing only. This idea is important for the approach to writing we've taken in this book. The Belenky et al. article makes a similar argument for writing as connected to life practice, this time through the lens of women's development theory. The authors claim that education connected to life experience is more accessible to women than evaluative, competitive, individualistic education because it fits better with our culture's training of women to be sympathetic and cooperative. Together, these two articles provide some good sociological reasons for considering a writing pedagogy based on small groups and aimed at invitations to a writer's life.

Freire, Paulo. 1985. "Chapter Two." In *Pedagogy of the Oppressed*, 57–74. 2nd ed. Translated by Myra Bergman Ramos. New York: Continuum.

This short manifesto is an indictment of the traditional lecture-style classroom—Freire calls it "banking" education, using the metaphor of the teacher making "deposits" into the minds of the students. In radical-Marxist terms, Freire shows how traditional education actually works against the self-reliance of the people it supposedly educates. He calls instead for a "problem-posing" education which identifies with the students' real problems all people in a culture face and which encourages a cooperative investigation of these problems. No matter how one feels about the Marxist background of Freire's thought, the analysis of education is provoking, especially as an indirect support for small-group pedagogy.

Gere, Anne Ruggles. 1987. *Writing Groups: History, Theory, Implications.* Carbondale: Southern Illinois University Press.

This monograph gives a useful overview of the way writing groups have developed in history, with particular attention paid to groups outside of academe. It's a useful source for placing classroom small groups into the wider context of writing groups throughout life.

Works Cited

Adams, Henry. 1931 [1919]. *The Education of Henry Adams*. New York: Modern Library.

Anson, Chris M., ed. 1989. *Writing and Response: Theory, Practice, and Research*. Urbana: National Council of Teachers of English.

Aptheker, Bettina. 1989. *Tapestries of Life: Women's Work, Women's Consciousness, and the Meaning of Daily Experience*. Amherst, MA: University of Massachusetts Press.

Atwell, Nancie. 1987. *In the Middle: Writing, Reading, and Learning with Adolescents*. Portsmouth, NH: Boynton/Cook-Heinemann.

———. 1991. *Side By Side: Essays on Teaching to Learn*. Portsmouth, NH: Heinemann Educational Books.

Bartholomae, David, and Anthony Petrosky. 1986. *Facts, Counterfacts, Artifacts: Theory and Method for a Reading and Writing Course*. Upper Montclair, NJ: Boynton/Cook.

———, eds. 1990. *Ways of Reading: An Anthology for Writers*. 2nd Ed. Boston: Bedford Books.

Bateson, Mary Catherine. 1989. *Composing a Life*. New York: Atlantic Monthly Press.

de Beauvoir, Simone. 1980. "Personal Freedom and Others." In *The Ethics of Ambiguity*, 35–73. Translated by Bernard Frechtman. New York: Citadel.

Belenky, Mary Field, Blythe McVicker Clinchy, Nancy Rule Goldberger, and Jill Mattuck Tarule. 1986. *Women's Ways of Knowing: The Development of Self, Mind, and Voice*. New York: Basic Books.

Berry, Wendell. 1988. "People, Land, and Community." In *Multi-Cultural Literacy*, edited by R. Simonson and S. Walker, 41–56. St. Paul: Graywolf Press.

Berthoff, Ann E. 1981. *The Making of Meaning: Metaphors, Models, and Maxims for Writing Teachers*. Upper Montclair, NJ: Boynton/Cook.

———. 1982. *Forming/Thinking/Writing: The Composing Imagination*. Upper Montclair, NJ: Boynton/Cook.

Bormann, Ernest. 1975. *Discussion and Group Methods: Theory and Practice*. 2nd ed. New York: Harper & Row.

———. 1990. *Small-Group Communication: Theory and Practice*. New York: Harper & Row, 1990.

Brooke, Robert. 1987. "Underlife and Writing Instruction." *College Composition and Communication* 38: 141–53.

———. 1991. *Writing and Sense of Self: Identity Negotiation in Writing Workshops*. Urbana: National Council of Teachers of English.

———, Tom O'Connor, and Ruth Mirtz. 1989. "Leadership in College Writing Groups." *Writing on the Edge* 1.1 (Fall): 66–86.

Brookes, Gerry. 1993. "Town Meetings." *College Composition and Communication* 44.1 (February): 88–92.

Brownmiller, Susan. 1975. *Against Our Will: Men, Women, and Rape.* New York: Simon and Schuster.

Bruffee, Kenneth. 1972. "A Way Out." *College English* 33: 457–70.

———. 1984. "Collaborative Writing and the Conversation of Mankind." *College English* 46: 635–52.

Calkins, Lucy McCormick. 1983. *Lessons from a Child: On the Teaching and Learning of Writing.* Exeter, NH: Heinemann Educational Books.

———. 1986. *The Art of Teaching Writing.* Portsmouth, NH: Heinemann.

———, with Shelley Harwayne. 1991. *Living between the Lines.* Portsmouth, NH: Heinemann.

Carter, Kathy. 1993. "The Place of Story in the Study of Teaching and Teacher Education." *Educational Researcher* 22(1): 5–12.

Didion, Joan. 1968. "On Keeping a Notebook." In *Slouching Toward Bethlehem,* 131–41. New York: Farrar, Strauss & Giroux.

Dreiser, Theodore. 1969 [1900]. *Sister Carrie.* Columbus, OH: Merrill.

Elbow, Peter. 1973. *Writing without Teachers.* New York: Oxford University Press.

———. 1981. *Writing with Power: Techniques for Mastering the Writing Process.* New York: Oxford University Press.

———. 1991a. "Reflections on Academic Discourse." *College English* 53: 135–55.

———. 1991b. *What Is English?* New York: Modern Language Association of America.

———, and Pat Belanoff. 1989. *A Community of Writers: A Workshop Course in Writing.* New York: Random House.

Faludi, Susan. 1991. *Backlash: The Undeclared War against American Women.* New York: Crown.

Fisher, B. Aubrey. 1980. *Small-Group Decision Making: Communication and the Group Process.* 2nd ed. New York: McGraw-Hill.

Flower, Linda. 1982. *Problem-Solving Strategies for Writing.* New York: Harcourt Brace Jovanovich.

Freire, Paulo. 1973. *Education for Critical Consciousness.* Translated by Myra Bergman Ramos. New York: Continuum.

———. 1985. *Pedagogy of the Oppressed.* 2nd ed. Translated by Myra Bergman Ramos. New York: Continuum.

Fulghum, Robert. 1988. *All I Really Needed to Know I Learned in Kindergarten.* New York: Villard.

———. 1989. *It Was on Fire When I Lay Down on It.* New York: Villard.

Gemmill, Gary, and Cal Wynkoop. 1991. "The Psychodynamics of Small-Group Transformation." *Small Group Research* 22.1 (February): 4–23.

Gere, Anne Ruggles. 1987. *Writing Groups: History, Theory, Implications.* Carbondale: Southern Illinois University Press.

Goffman, Erving. 1961. *Asylums: Essays on the Social Situation of Mental Patients and Other Inmates.* Chicago: Aldine.

———. 1963. *Stigma: Notes on the Management of Spoiled Identity.* Englewood Cliff, NJ: Prentice-Hall.

Goldberg, Natalie. 1986. *Writing Down the Bones: Freeing the Writer within.* Boston: Shambala.

Graves, Donald H. 1984. *A Researcher Learns to Write: Selected Articles and Monographs.* Portsmouth, NH: Heinemann.

Harris, Joseph. 1989. "The Idea of Community in the Study of Writing." *College Composition and Communication* 40.1 (February): 11–22.

Haswell, Richard H. 1991. *Gaining Ground in College Writing: Tales of Development and Interpretation.* Dallas: Southern Methodist University Press.

Heath, Shirley Brice. 1983. *Ways With Words: Language, Life, and Work in Communities and Classrooms.* New York: Cambridge University Press.

hooks, bell. 1989. *Talking Back: Thinking Feminist, Thinking Black.* Boston: South End Press, 1989.

Jones, Tom. 1991. "Walking Down the Road Toward Learning." In Elbow 1991b, 264–65.

Kelly, Lou. 1972. *From Dialogue to Discourse: An Open Approach to Competence and Creativity.* London: Scott, Foresman.

Kuhn, Thomas S. 1970. *The Structure of Scientific Revolutions.* 2nd Ed. Chicago: University of Chicago Press.

Limbaugh, Rush. 1992. *The Way Things Ought to Be.* New York: Pocket Books.

Lloyd-Jones, Richard, and Andrea A. Lunsford, eds. 1989. *The English Coalition Conference: Democracy through Language.* Urbana: National Council of Teachers of English/Modern Language Association of America.

McMillan, Terry. 1992. *Waiting to Exhale.* New York: Viking.

Moffett, James. 1968. *Teaching the Universe of Discourse.* Boston: Houghton Mifflin.

Murray, Donald M. 1978. "Internal Revision." In *Research on Composing: Points of Departure,* edited by Charles R. Cooper and Lee Odell, 85—104. Urbana: National Council of Teachers of English.

———. 1985. *A Writer Teaches Writing.* 2nd Ed. Boston: Houghton Mifflin.

———. 1990. *Write to Learn.* 3rd Ed. Fort Worth: Holt, Rinehart and Winston.

North, Stephen M. 1987. *The Making of Knowledge in Composition: Portrait of an Emerging Field.* Upper Montclair, NJ: Boynton/Cook.

Rand, Ayn. 1957. *Atlas Shrugged.* New York: Random House.

Rief, Linda. 1992. *Seeking Diversity: Language Arts with Adolescents.* Portsmouth, NH: Boynton/Cook-Heinemann.

Roberts, W. Rhys, trans. 1954. *The Rhetoric,* by Aristotle. New York: Modern Library.

Roebke, Jenny. 1977. "English in the Context of Community." *Nebraska English Counselor* (Fall): n.p.

Romano, Tom. 1987. *Clearing The Way: Working with Teenage Writers.* Portsmouth, NH: Heinemann.

Rothwell, Dan. 1992. *In Mixed Company: Small-Group Communication*. New York: Harcourt Brace Jovanovich.

Scieszka, John. 1989. *The True Story of the Three Little Pigs (as Told by A. Wolf)*. New York: Viking.

Shor, Ira. 1987. *Critical Teaching and Everyday Life*. Chicago: University of Chicago Press.

Spear, Karen. 1988. *Sharing Writing: Peer-Response Groups in English Classes*. Portsmouth, NH: Boynton/Cook-Heinemann.

Stein, Gertrude. 1973 [1909]. *Three Lives: Stories of the Good Anna, Melanctha, and the Gentle Lena*. New York: Vintage.

Tannen, Deborah. 1986. *That's Not What I Meant! How Conversational Style Makes or Breaks Your Relations with Others*. New York: Ballantine.

———. 1990. *You Just Don't Understand: Women and Men in Conversation*. New York: Ballantine.

Thomas, Dene, and Gordon Thomas. 1989. "The Use of Rogerian Reflection in Small-Group Writing Conferences." In Anson, 114–26.

Tompkins, Jane. 1992. "The Way We Live Now." *Change* 24.6 (November/December): 13–19.

Trimbur, John. 1989. "Consensus and Difference in Collaborative Learning." *College English* 51.6 (October): 606–16.

Tuckman, B. 1965. "Developmental Sequences in Small Groups." *Psychological Bulletin* 63: 384–99.

Vonnegut, Kurt. 1981. *Palm Sunday*. New York: Dell.

Young, Richard E., Alton L. Becker, and Kenneth L. Pike. 1970. *Rhetoric: Discovery and Change*. New York: Harcourt Brace Jovanovich.

Index

Authors

Robert Brooke is associate professor of English at the University of Nebraska–Lincoln, where he teaches writing classes at all levels and works with the Nebraska Writing Project. Some of his recent publications include "Underlife and Writing Instruction" (1987), which won the Richard Braddock Award, and *Writing and Sense of Self* (NCTE, 1991).

Ruth Mirtz is assistant professor of English at Florida State University and director of the First-Year Writing Program. Before moving to Florida, she directed the Writing Lab at the University of Nebraska. She has presented papers at CCCC and MLA and published in *Writing on the Edge, ADE Bulletin,* and *Composition Studies.* She plans to continue her work with small groups in writing classes and is currently investigating first-year college students' concepts of identity and authority.

Rick Evans is assistant professor of English at the University of Nebraska–Lincoln, where he teaches linguistics and works with the teacher education program. He has recent articles in *Discourse Processes* and *Teacher Research* and is currently investigating the folklore of pheasant hunting on the Great Plains.